Depression
as a
Spiritual
Journey

First published by O Books, 2009
O Books is an imprint of John Hunt Publishing Ltd., The Bothy, Deershot Lodge, Park Lane, Ropley,
Hants, SO24 0BE, UK
office1@o-books.net
www.o-books.net

Distribution in:	South Africa
	Alternative Books
UK and Europe	altbook@peterhyde.co.za
Orca Book Services	Tel: 021 555 4027 Fax: 021 447 1430
orders@orcabookservices.co.uk	
Tel: 01202 665432 Fax: 01202 666219	Text copyright Stephanie Sorrell 2008
Int. code (44)	
	Design: Stuart Davies
USA and Canada	Cover illustration: Hanne Jahr
NBN	
custserv@nbnbooks.com	ISBN: 978 1 84694 223 5
Tel: 1 800 462 6420 Fax: 1 800 338 4550	
	All rights reserved. Except for brief quotations
Australia and New Zealand	in critical articles or reviews, no part of this
Brumby Books	book may be reproduced in any manner without
sales@brumbybooks.com.au	prior written permission from the publishers.
Tel: 61 3 9761 5535 Fax: 61 3 9761 7095	
	The rights of Stephanie Sorrell as author have
Far East (offices in Singapore, Thailand,	been asserted in accordance with the
Hong Kong, Taiwan)	Copyright, Designs and Patents Act 1988.
Pansing Distribution Pte Ltd	
kemal@pansing.com	A CIP catalogue record for this book is available
Tel: 65 6319 9939 Fax: 65 6462 5761	from the British Library.

Printed by Digital Book Print

Depression
as a
Spiritual
Journey

Stephanie Sorrell, MA

BOOKS

Winchester, UK
Washington, USA

CONTENTS

Dedication   viii

Acknowledgement   x

Foreword   1

Introduction   3

PART I

Chapter 1: Asking the Right Questions   13

Chapter 2: What is Depression?   15

Depression as an Illness of Being   19

Moderate to Major Depression   23

Seasonal Affective Disorder   27

Bipolar Disorder   29

Dark Night of the Soul and Creative Depression   34

Loss of Spiritual Connection   34

Chapter 3: Depression as a Spiritual Journey   36

Chapter 4: The Meaning of Suffering   42

The Three Levels of Suffering   44

Suffering through the Lens of the Major Religions   46

Suffering as Service   49

Chapter 5: Persephone and the Underworld   52

The Story   54

Will and Choice   56

Unpacking the Myth   58

A Moral Compass   66

The Light in the Darkness   67

PART II

Chapter 6: Tools on the Journey   69

Medical Intervention   69

My Own Experience 70

The Healing Field 71

Serotonin and Depression 73

Neurotransmitters and the Role of Neurons 76

Depression and the Brain 79

Glial Cells – the Glue 80

Antidepressants 81

Side Effects 88

Why Medication doesn't Always Work 89

What to do when Medication does Work 90

The Difficulty in Accepting Medication 91

Chapter 7: The Roots of Psychology 99

Psychodynamic Therapy 102

Cognitive Behavior Therapy 107

Humanistic Counseling 112

Transpersonal Psychology 114

Jungian Analytical Therapy 117

Post Jungians and Creative Depression 124

Jung and Assagioli 124

Chapter 8: My Journey into Psychosynthesis 127

Psychiatrist, Mountaineer and Mystic 131

As Above, so Below 133

PART III

Chapter 9: Going Deeper 137

Sea Journey as Metaphor 138

The Odyssey 140

Chapter 10: Spiritual Emergency to Spiritual Emergence 144

Stanislav Grof, A Psychiatrist with Insight 149

A Psychotic Episode or Spiritual Emergency 154

Spiritual Emergency and the Dark Night of the Soul 157

Distinctions between the Self and the Superconscious 164

Distinctions between Mystical Experience and Schizophrenia 164

Spiritual and Global Emergency Today 165

Chapter 11: The Dark Night of the Soul   167
Teresa of Avila   169
St John of the Cross   176
Grace   178

Chapter 12: Defining the Dark Night   180
Dark Night of the Senses   181
Dark Night of the Spirit   186

Chapter 13: Depression and the Dark Night of the Soul   191

Chapter 14: Treasure and Creative Darkness   197
Creativity as Process   204

PART IV
Chapter 15: How to be with someone who is Depressed   215

Chapter 16: Understanding Suicide   223
"I Have Lost my Angel."   223
Shame   224
Suicide in the Young   225
Suicide in the Elderly   226
Mindsets about Suicide   227
Suicide Bombers   229

Chapter 17: How to be with a Suicidal Person   232
From Doing to Being   232
As a Spiritual Journey   234
The Gift   235

Conclusion   238
Glossary   240
References   244

Dedication

To all who suffer depression in its diversity of forms and those who work to alleviate and bring insight and meaning to those who are depressed.

This light....
I hold in my hands is intangible,
Beautiful and mysterious
As water from some crystal brook,
or snowdrops in the winter sun,
or the pale egg breaking in the waiting nest.

This light...
I have dredged deeply to find
As the tree's tap root
Quarries far into the soil.
Long have I journeyed for it.
Traversing forbidding lands where
My fears battled to crush my truth.
Wearily, I have sought it through endless
Nights that could not promise dawn.

This light...
I have died for once, twice,
Many times.
Yet...
This light in my hands,
Beautiful, radiant and eternal
Has always been mine.
It is ever I who have travelled far from it.

This light…
That I now hold, waiting to come
Bursting through every heart and pouring
Through every stranger's eyes, will never
Let me go. Not ever.
This I know…
This I believe…

Stephanie Sorrell

Acknowledgement

First and foremost I would like to thank Hanne Jahr, my best friend, who has painstakingly read through my work in various stages and whose suggestions have been invaluable. Also I am thrilled with her much coveted painting on the cover.

I would also like to thank Roger Evans, my thesis tutor and director of the Institute of Psychosynthesis, for suggesting that he would like to see me expand the work into a book. I am especially indebted to his taught components of the courses, *The Nature of Suffering* and *Spiritual Emergency and Emergence*, for bringing the work so alive and enabling me to see my suffering in a meaningful context.

Additionally, I would like to thank Anne Welsh for her unwavering acceptance of my depressed condition throughout much of the training, and who never gave up believing in me while I was in hospital and whose empathy was tangible.

I would also like to acknowledge the thoughts, ideas and especially support from the students I trained with, particularly those known as 'the sisters' in the applied program: Marguerite Falvey, Heather Jenkins, Chris Roberts, Heather Samson and Graham Kean.

Also my gratitude goes to Theodora Bell who, over four years, became my friend and introduced me to the deer of Richmond Park and gave me somewhere to sleep along with mouth watering dishes during those endless training weekends.

I am also indebted to the work of the late psychiatrist, Gerald May, in his skilful unpacking of the 'Dark Night of the Soul'. I have found his work on the subject, *The Dark Night of the Soul,* invaluable.

I have been ever heartened by Jane Sorbi's stalwart belief in the theme of the book from the start and her constant presence throughout my writing of it. I am also grateful for Colum Hayward's helpful suggestions in the beginning.

I would also like to thank Mavis Gregson, a friend of Michelle Lovric's, one of my endorsees, who just popped in, asked to read my book, and gave me critical but highly valuable feedback on the manuscript during the final editing process.

Finally, I would like to thank John Hunt at O Books for seeing potential in this project and taking me on.

Foreword

Once in a while there comes a book that fundamentally challenges and transforms the prevailing mindset within a particular field. For example, David Bohm's seminal work, *The Implicate Order*, in quantum physics and Rupert Sheldrake's, *Presence of the Past*, in biology, have done this and have opened their fields to new levels of insight and exploration.

In psychological health and particularly within the complex and difficult field of depression we now have such a book. In re-contextualizing, *Depression as a Spiritual Journey*, Stephanie Sorrells's serious and radical book, gives patients and health professionals a handbook of hope.

I feel privileged to have been invited to write the foreword to this important new perspective on depression; privileged, because it allows me to put my professional psychotherapeutic experience behind the premise that depression is a spiritual journey. Important new perspective, because this context provides individuals – who as Stephanie says 'live with and work within the field of depression' – with a fundamentally new context to work through many forms of depression, one that potentially brings new levels of meaning to their suffering and the hope that transforms.

While acknowledging the deep-seated historical etiology of some depressive conditions, she powerfully positions depression as a condition of psychospiritual pathology, whereby the individual's disconnection from Self and loss of spiritual meaning reverberates through suffering at the level of soul as well as the personality.

1

In this way, rather than 'help, fix or try to cure' she help us understand how to 'be with depression' and allow the reconnection to Self.

> *And I said to my soul be still and let the dark come upon you, which shall be the darkness of God.*
> T.S Eliot, East Coker

In reading this book I invite the reader, whether sufferer or professional, to do the exercises in chapter one on how to ask questions. Please don't skip them, they are so seminal to the thesis that Stephanie Sorrell develops in the rest of her book and takes us beyond. In these exercises we journey, as she says, beyond the 'traditional questions that belong to our fix-it culture. These are: How can we fix depression? How can we cure it? How can we overcome it?'

Through learning to 'ask the right questions' she takes the sufferer to another level of meaning and experience of depression and provides a platform to help the reader understand a psychospiritual context for the different levels of suffering, of personality (historical), of soul (search for meaning), of Self (facing the struggle of how to live with knowing love and that we are interconnected to all beings).

Those of us trained in Roberto Assagioli's psychosynthesis – essentially a psychology of hope – have been fortunate to have lived and worked within a psychospiritual psychology. This important work continues that tradition and will, I believe, bring a new chapter in understanding and 'being with many forms of depression'.

Roger H Evans
Psychotherapist and co-founder of the
Institute of Psychosynthesis, London

Introduction

The aim of this work is to explore and give meaning to depressive illness by bringing it into a psychospiritual context. This is the ability to see what is happening on both a spiritual and psychological level. Rather than spirituality being exclusive to a particular religion or belief system, I understand it to be the connectivity that runs through all religions and all people. Spirituality is the grace that connects us; it is the light that shines through and includes all difference.

The purpose of this work is not about finding a cure or a solution for depression, but rather in validating it as an essential spiritual journey that is undertaken on both an individual and collective level. It is about the often harrowing loss of spiritual connection through descent into darkness and depression. But it is also about the rebirth and resurrection of the spiritual light within by entering the void which is essentially creative and accessing the inner treasures. This seems almost a paradox – that a condition which shadows the life with such a deep sense of futility can become a container for so much meaning.

More than anything, it is about developing a radically different relationship with depressive illness by bringing it into the context of soul. By including and integrating the soul we can bridge the split between body and mind, psychopathology and medical science. The soul, this exiled component of our being, enters incarnation and 'suffers' the meaning within each life experience. The soul, the mediator between spirit and matter is the servant of the spirit and is crucified in matter, just as the clay molded by the potter is surrendered to the fire of the kiln in

3

order to attain completion.

My particular interest in this area emerges from a lifelong struggle with depressive illness which, again, reflects an identical historical struggle that has replicated again and again throughout my family. Since I am the last member of my family, I feel responsible for what feels like redeeming some long buried ancestral treasure which has too much value to be forgotten and bring it to light and consciousness. In doing this I want to break the cycle of shame which has haunted my family where suicide and alcoholism have displaced the value of this very internal experience. From a psychosocial perspective, what has taken place in my own family is a metaphor for what is escalating and taking place on a collective level and, as the World Health Authority asserts, is reaching epidemic proportions. Writing this book has enabled me to ground some of the insights I have gained both on a personal level and within my field of research through a wide range of literature and through my training in psychosynthesis psychology.

A vision haunts me from my late twenties when, during an acute depression, I was praying and became aware of a dark figure of an angel in the room. When I asked why it was dark, it drew back its cloak and I was blinded by an incredible light. This, to me, exemplifies 'the light in the darkness'. As there is an intimate relationship between suffering and the soul, as demonstrated in my chapter, *The Meaning of Suffering*, there is also a complementary connection between darkness and light.

In a purely physical sense, we can understand this connection through using the eye as a metaphor for marrying the light and darkness. It is because the pupil is black that we can receive the light. And in the centre of the candle flame lays the shadow. Sunlight in nature causes a lacework of shadows. In art, the efficacy of a painting is often held within the subtle interplay of light and shadow, rather than shape and detail. In fact, it is the light and shadow which lend the painting life and depth.

Scientifically, we have only just discovered, in the last twenty years, that most of the matter in the universe is unknown. Scientist, Rupert Sheldrake, further asserts that 'dark matter turns out to constitute ninety-nine percent of the matter in the Universe.' In fact, he adds, 'the cosmos seems to be grounded in dark matter. It seems that dark matter underlies everything.'

In the context of depression, this is fascinating. Yet this fundamental connection between darkness and light in a metaphysical sense is something we have lost sight of in our obsession with perceiving all matter on a superficial, horizontal level, rather than a vertical more penetrating level. Until we reconnect with the myths our ancestors emerged from, we will always fall short in our inclusion of spiritual growth being core to our development and continuation as a race.

In the mystical tradition, Matthew Fox, minister and writer, reminds us that the 'Godhead is dark'. If we have no language for mystical experience today, we can only pathologize it with our insubstantial tools of understanding and thus alienate ourselves even further from our spiritual source.

And here I want to suggest that not all depression is pathological, or solely pathological, but a crucial and natural component of our spiritual journey. I see it mirroring an archetypal descent that many mystics, visionaries and shamans made cross-culturally in the past and which, fortunately, has been recorded as part of our heritage. For example, Malidoma Patrice Some's compelling portrayal of initiation and underworld experiences as part of his re-admission back into the West African Dagara tribe became an integral part of his self development. He describes how, in his time away from the tribe in the outside world; 'I had grown away from myself into a mould that tried to make me into someone I wasn't.' After his initiation, he said 'I grew into myself. The problems I had became resolved as I entered into my true nature.'

One of the major symptoms of depression is a crippling sense of isolation, alienation and separation. 'Depression, at its root, is a disease of disconnection,' sociologist, David Karp, stresses in his book, *Speaking of Sadness*. This is experienced on both a psychosocial and a psychospiritual level where one, simultaneously, feels a distinct lack of connection to daily life and a profound loss of connection with God or any other spiritual source.

'The greatest affliction of the sorrowful soul in this state,' writes St John of the Cross, 'is the thought that God has abandoned it.' This is also the crucifixion agony of Christ; 'Father, why has Thou forsaken me?' St John of the Cross referred to this as 'The Dark Night of the Soul' and wrote lengthily on this, not as an illness, but an essential component of the journey – as a descent in service of a more intimate connection with God. This process is cogently delineated in *The Divine Comedy* where Dante, the writer and protagonist, is led by his guide, Vigil, down into purgatory before ascending with his second guide, Beatrice, to paradise. Interestingly, St John of the Cross writes about the often destructive effects of so called 'spiritual directors' on this descent. He claimed that very few initiates had the will, longing, strength or awareness to engage fully in this journey and so therefore had no real comprehension of it. His comparison of these 'counselors' with Job's comforters rings even more true today as many 'spiritually aware' people too easily impart glib and questionable advice about negative states of being. At least, however, the initiate is given ample opportunity to develop discrimination through wisdom which is a vital skill on the spiritual journey. As spirituality can often harbor deeply repressed narcissistic tendencies, real guidance, in the form of therapists who can fully facilitate another's passage through their 'dark night', is hard to find.

The work of Czech psychiatrist, Stanislav Grof, presents some interesting insights after extensive work with clients experiencing non-ordinary states of consciousness. He found that a number of his client's symptoms, despite their similarity to ones experienced by psychotics and schizophrenics, maintained full awareness of what was taking place inwardly. Beyond their very real physical, emotional and mental symptoms of distress, they maintained a startling lucidity and were in full command of their internal experience. The more Grof worked with these people, the more he saw that they were in a state of 'spiritual emergency' which was, as he admitted, an inner crisis. He pointed out that in Chinese calligraphy; crisis was made up of two glyphs: 'opportunity' and 'danger'. He said that within this state the client felt separated, exiled from the Divine. If he facilitated this process without trying to label or change it, the client came through and afterwards experienced a deeper unity with God, whereas preceding the experience they had only been aware of an inner aridity and emptiness. The 'spiritual emergency' experience had somehow brought them closer to a sense of the divine. I explore the whole concept of spiritual emergency and 'spiritual emergence' alongside the 'Dark Night of the Soul' in depth in this book.

I do feel today, because of the way we have exiled soul and depth from our worldview in our Western preoccupation with materialism and the future, we stand at a critical juncture in our psychological and spiritual evolution. For many of us, the only way forward is down and back, and in Ken Wilber's terms 'integrating and including' the past along with what we may tend to see as the less palatable aspect of our nature. To do that we must be prepared to expand our view on depressive illness and bring it into the framework of a spiritual disorder that is looking for depth and meaning. Until we do, our cultural inheritance of shame and pathology will keep us out of relationship with what it has to offer, rather than what we can gain. We should ask ourselves instead: *What does this depression have to offer in the way of gifts and insight?* Within the Christian tradition of the nativity, the Christ light is enacted at the darkest time of the year.

Similarly, depressive illness is reaching peak levels at a time when there is a critical need for Western people to realign with the purpose, meaning and values of our true spiritual nature.

The Jungian analyst, Esther Harding, compared depression with the Wilderness, which is the soul experience of being in a wasteland: an inhospitable place where there appears to be no life and nothing can grow. Building on this, I have found the wilderness to be part of a natural cyclical phase replicating in nature. Here, I can use the model of a tree as a metaphor for this cycle. The wilderness corresponds to a saturnine winter period, when the leaves and fruit have been stripped away. It marks a point of desolation, of entropy. The interface between the inner and outer world no longer holds. The way through is made initially by acceptance and then using this 'barren' period to reflect on the past and see oneself in a new way. Contemplation and aspiration are the stages that follow reflection. This reflective passage which focuses more on 'being' rather than 'doing' certainly saw the Christian Desert Fathers through their long vigil.

Practically, I have started at ground level to give insight into the history of depressive illness, our mindsets and where they have come from, to *The Meaning of Suffering*, through to *The Treasure* and the necessary distinctions which need to be made between spiritual emergency and spiritual emergence and to the spiritual journey itself.

As spirit is ever struggling to come into form through matter/mother, both ground and spirit are essential components of any work. When I talk about ground in this book, I am talking about bringing insights into form and into matter in order to work with them in our life. Spirit cannot come into form unless there is ground to germinate and work within. It doesn't matter how profound and wonderful our visions and ideas are, unless we can ground or earth them they cannot be implemented in the world. I have found that this is why, after a period of spiritual illumination, there is a period of disillusionment and descent.

Yet descent is valuable; it deepens insight and is the polar opposite of the rarefied air on the mountain top. The incredible thing is that God or the Divine is often found in the darkness. Matthew Fox writes 'The light in us increases and paradoxically so, as we go more deeply into the dark, as we sink.' He further suggests that a lot of our addictions are efforts to intervene with the darkness that is happening.

One of the issues that compromise our understanding of depression is that emotional and mental dis-ease become clumped together under one fuzzy heading. For example, what is the difference between melancholia and clinical depression? Why do people today suffer from an assortment of depressions rather than good old-fashioned melancholia which was once seen more as a character quality rather than a personality deficit? What is the difference between psychosis and depression or the 'Dark Night of the Soul' and depression? Is there a difference between a psychotic episode and spiritual emergency? What criteria do we use to make these distinctions? I have endeavored in this work to define some of these distinctions and unearth many of our mindsets that shape our ambivalent attitude to depression; mindsets that are so dominant that we may have become blind and unconscious to them.

I also unravel the threads of the Greek Myth, *Persephone and the Underworld*. This is a cyclical drama which is re-enacted both cross-culturally as well as on a very real level within the cyclical passage of the seasons when the long winter months, leached of life and activity, finally give way to spring. This corresponds to Persephone's return from her long internment in the underworld and her re-emergence with the rising of the sap and the blessings of new life being restored to the earth. This annual cyclical passage from a place of innocence and bliss to loss and imprisonment, and crucifixion to resurrection and new growth, is a re-enactment of the soul's journey. If we can refer to this as an organic template underpinning our own process, we have a map to follow, one that is natural as it is arduous, yet potentially empowering.

Descents often lead to treasure, and this I open out later in my chapter, *The Treasure*, and explore how depression can fuel the alchemical fires of creativity and explain the creative process in progress in our lives and our fears around it. I also include how the creative process is inexorably linked to the natural environment and how our treatment of this is a metaphor for how we are damning up our creativity in collusion with societal values.

The chapter, *Understanding Suicide*, unmasks the hidden problem of suicide and gives what I feel to be a moving portrayal of the despair that drives people to suicide. This also sensitively covers suicide bombers and the high values which direct their intention, yet fails when it becomes implemented on the level of the personality. I have included two chapters which are key to anyone working with someone who is depressed or suicidal, which emerged from a call from therapist colleagues to address this in my book. I have named these, *How to be with someone who is Depressed?* and *How to be with someone who is Suicidal?*

The inclusion of the chapter, *Tools on the Journey*, introduces the use of medication and counseling as valid and therapeutic ways to 'hold' and lend a measure of stability through internal crisis. Medical intervention may come as a surprise to some who believe that spiritual healing is the one and only avenue of relief. The intervention of spiritual healing can simply manifest through being 'guided' to the right therapist or right doctor. I believe a lot of this initial resistance to medication stems from a natural fear of becoming dependent on medication or using it to mask deeper issues that should be faced. If we accept that all life is held within a spiritual matrix, we understand that there is little difference between alternative medicine and conventional medicine in that they both are informed by the same intention to heal. For these reasons I have referred to my own journey through medication and counseling in the appropriate sections, after trying to deal with it solely on a spiritual level.

I need to explain here some of the terminology I shall use, although there is a glossary of terms at the back of this book. My references to the 'Self' with a capital 'S' refers to our highest nature, pure spirit. The Self is spirit in matter, yet speaks and makes its presence known through all levels of being and manifestation. In psychosynthesis psychology 'Self is' and 'becomes manifest' through a gradual awakening of the 'I' in a human being. This 'I' refers to the observing self, the part of us that appears to watch the world, the behavior of others and ourselves with interest rather than judgment. Most of the time we are only vaguely aware of a sense of Self and will have a deepening experience of being a detached observer as we view the world through the lens of the 'I'. Those of us who become easily seduced by the mind and become too strongly identified with the emotional body will be aware of the pushes and pulls of the personality which may come from the level of the ego. In simpler terms, the ego is a vehicle through which we learn to function in the world, sometimes in defense or through a slow systematic whittling away of the personality from frustration and wounding. In essence, we are creating our pearl, strengthening our 'I' so that it can choose between identifying with the ego or the Self. Much of the material in this book is about developing a dialogue between the I and the Self. What I hope I can illustrate here is that Self can speak through the depression and illness, even though the existential alienation from the Divine is profound. It speaks as much today as it did in the time of St John of the Cross and St Teresa of Avila in the 17th century.

I always remember the words I heard six years ago when I began my journey into finding a meaning and context for depression. These were 'The Self speaks through the symptoms.' And even if the symptoms appear to be trapped in the personality or egoic level, it is still the Self speaking. I remember this when I am in distress or am with another in distress – that the Self, the Spirit, is speaking through those very same symptoms. And especially today, where there are so many symptoms of global and personal distress, the Self is speaking...

PART I

Chapter 1

Asking the Right Questions

The only real voyage of discovery consists not in seeking new lands
but seeing with new eyes.
Marcel Proust

Before reading this page it is worth having some crayons, paints or pastels and paper ready.

Children ask a lot of questions because they know questions open up consciousness. And as our experience of children supports this, we know that one question leads to another – and another… It's hard work answering this never ending barrage of questions because we have to think and translate what we know into digestible food for the young mind. Sadly, as we become older, many of us lose the ability to ask questions. In our minds we become inflexible and bogged down with fixed mindsets and beliefs about the world, each other and ourselves. The questions we do ask are perfunctory ones like determining times and dates for meetings and events, monetary costs of services and information we need to know before investing in a future project. If we do ask questions, we have forgotten to ask the right ones.

When looking at depression the questions we tend to ask are traditional ones that belong to our fix-it culture. These are: How can we fix depression? How can we cure it? How can we overcome it?

These questions send us in the direction of cure after cure. Some of them work for a while, others don't. Not only do we relegate depression to being an 'it' but we perceive it as an anomaly that needs to be cured.

If we can learn to ask the right questions then we open the doors of perception and the subject we are addressing takes on a different context and holds potential that we can utilize and harness.

For example think about this question:

What does depression serve? Or, How has depression served me?

Be aware of what happens inside your mind. *What happens on a bodily level?*

How does this make you feel?

Open the question out further to reveal the seed kernels of other questions.

What qualities has my depression given me?

What do these qualities look like?

If you find your insights difficult to articulate, try using your writing and drawing tools to sketch what you may not be able to put into words.

When you have addressed these questions and insights close your eyes and imagine that your depression is a tree and this tree is an aspect of you. Take a few minutes to be aware of this tree. What sort of branches does it have, if any? Are there leaves or fruit? What sort of climate does it grow within? Do your friends and colleagues know this tree? Do you value this tree or are you ashamed of it?

When you have done this, put this drawing/painting in a safe place until the section of the book that invites you to re-examine it. You don't have to remember this for now. Let this journey remember this initial template for you.

But now we will look at what depression is by looking at some of the main types of depression.

Chapter 2

What is Depression?

I am writing this in the midst of the radical new mental health proposal drawn up by the government to address the escalating mental health issues in Britain today. Weighing up the cost of depression related illnesses in the health service; the government has decided to train 10,000 mental health professionals in the next seven years in Cognitive Behavior Therapy (see Chapter 7). The training would take the form of intensive training programs in hospitals and universities over this period of time. Additionally, The World Health Organization (WHO) has predicted that by the year 2020 depression will account for the second largest burden of disease. The first is heart disease, yet evidence is emerging all the time that depression is one of the conditions that underlie cardiac problems. Not only that, but even adult-onset diabetes occurs more often in the depressed. These statistics and observations are not just confined to the Western world, but abound globally, regardless of ethnic background, age or class.

Where, in the past, depression has remained largely in the province of adulthood, with the average age of onset being 30 years, at the time of writing this the average age of onset has changed quite drastically to 14 or 15 years old. For this reason some 20 schools in Britain are teaching 'happiness classes' where young people can learn to approach emotional and mental problems in a psychologically beneficial way. In fact, US-based psychologist, Dr Martin Seligman, found that after conducting a

$2.8m three year study in the United States, children who had been taught 'positive psychology' performed better in class and had a greater sense of wellbeing.

All of us will have encountered depression in a variety of shapes and forms amongst our colleagues, friends and family and are therefore affected in some way. From these experiences and encounters we will have formed a number of ideas and prejudices about depression which enable us to make sense of it. At the very least, it is an incapacitating condition which undermines our ability to enjoy life. Further along this continuum depression jeopardizes our ability to function as a human being. We see that physically, sleep and appetite are thrown out of kilter and there is a deep underlying sense of exhaustion that eclipses all activities. Psychologically, the mind is plagued by an endless litany of negative thoughts. Emotionally, one is awash with deep, often unconscious, anxieties and unremitting feelings of guilt about being in such a reduced state which give rise to an incoming tide of irresolvable shame. In the grip of self-punishing thoughts there is little refuge in the medley of self help books which serve to make the person feel even more inadequate because, it seems, the harder he/she tries, the more resistant becomes the ability to emerge from the 'slough of despondency', described so eloquently by John Bunyan's *Pilgrim's Progress*. Perhaps more excruciatingly painful than anything is the sense of disconnection which manifests in feeling emotionally alienated from others and spiritually exiled from God or a spiritual source. Biologically, disconnection is experienced in the brain as thoughts slow down and the body becomes so lethargic that the simplest task or decision is rendered impossible.

Despite all the research into depression from Hippocrates in 400BC to modern psychiatry, psychotherapy, psychopharmacology, electro-convulsive treatment (ECT) and various forms of healing, we are still no nearer to *accepting* this condition. If anything, our cultural obsession to fix, transform and get rid of depression is as powerful as ever. And, although some depression may respond to any of the above treatments, its value and underlying cause remains as evasive and elusive as ever. We can accept and understand, to a certain degree, the sort of depression that is reactive and manifests in response to loss of any sort on a professional and financial level. Disappointment and sorrow inevitably follow in the wake of bereavement of a dear friend or loss of a significant relationship. This is a natural reaction, but what is harder to accept is a depression that descends for no apparent reason, cauterizing the flow of life and taking up uninvited residence for weeks, months or even years.

We have, effectively, devised a number of ways to make sense of this unwelcome visitor: Psychoanalysis, for example, looks towards the childhood and faulty parenting to identify a cause; physiologically, we can blame faulty genes and biochemical imbalances that affect serotonin and dopamine levels in the brain; a plethora of innovative and exciting information is emerging from the field of medical science which supports the theory that depression has a biological cause, lending credibility to the fast growing area of psychopharmacology and the antidepressants which affect the serotonergic circuits in the brain (see Chapter 6).

But as medical science is fast making headway towards concocting an effective panacea for depressive illness, the spiritual voice of our times remains remarkably silent on the subject. Even the new-age thinking concerning past life theories of pain and suffering and karmic retribution have dropped into the background. This is not a comfortable silence though and my theory is the general ambience of shame that surrounds depression in the spiritual milieu is the reason why. It is as if, as Dr Jonathon Zeuss says 'Truly spiritual people do not become depressed, or that depression is a sin, or that it is the result of sin and guilt, or bad karma, and so on. They might think depression can never be used by God as a means for personal growth.'

The outlook that embraces this zealous positive thinking model can resort to 'spiritual flight' and cut off from the valuable insight that depression can provide. This is the polar opposite extreme of wallowing in the depths of emotional entanglement with childhood history, instead of seeking to integrate and heal that area of pain which can be the negative side of psychoanalyses.

No single one of these therapeutic models, whether in the form of psychoanalyses, medication or fostering a wholly spiritual outlook, holds the answer in itself. The answer lies in all of the theories to a greater or lesser extent. The relevance of each varies from person to person and may be practiced individually along a continuum or used in conjunction with each other; for example, counseling and pharmacology. Some people may pursue the medical model for a period of years and find relief and efficacy in orthodox medication, but later on choose to explore further afield and complement this with psychotherapy or spiritual practice. Others, who have gained some understanding of themselves psychologically, may find further relief through medication or belonging to a spiritual network or community. Healing and relief can manifest through any therapeutic medium, but if one works reasonably well, it doesn't mean that the others are wrong or ineffective for everyone. Psychopharmacology, psychotherapy and spiritual counseling are all valid routes of healing for the depressed person because we are fundamentally all psychophysical, psychological, psychosocial and psychospiritual beings.

Within difference is tension and in our culture we often interpret tension as negative, rather than being proactive and transformative. Our fear and dislike of change and discomfort make us want to split off from an opinion, or a way of being that is different to our own. In this way, something potentially good becomes tarnished by its own emerging difference. And because we are unable to tolerate the difference, we split off from it, whether it is a person, way of life or culture. The learning and growth *is in the tension of holding that difference.*

Let's look at depression, this uncomfortable difference that we want to exile both in ourselves and each other.

Depression as an Illness of Being

Depression, contrary to our frenetic culture of 'getting and spending' is principally about *being*. In this sense it is the shadow side of a civilization polarized towards *doing*. And it is worth reminding ourselves that we are human beings. It is within our nature to be and become the receptacles of life, vessels of wisdom carrying the distillation of life experience. Without this essentially creative way of being we cannot make sense of our experiences. We hurry through our lives without taking time to draw breath or refuel. Consequently, we are hungry, thirsty and spiritually impoverished.

Living in a world of polarity where opposites hold either end of life's continuum, an over emphasis on activity and doing sets itself up for a descent, often cataclysmic, into a deficit of being. Evolution and entropy lie in juxtaposition and are integral components of the cycle of birth, death and resurrection which is so prevalent in the natural world. The concept of being, contrary to our Westernized perception, is transformative and potent. Within the context of our frenetic lifestyle – where even our holidays, demoted from 'holy days', are dynamic and packed with activity – the only way we can experience being is through illness, dis-ease and loss. And because we are encouraged to be merchants of material possessions, outward skills and accomplishment, we have so much to lose. In fact, as a culture, we set ourselves up for loss. However, it is through illness, dis-ease, loss and hunger that we begin to experience what Buddhists refer to as the emptiness that underlies all life. Not a negative emptiness which has been conceived in the West as a kind of hell, but a creative and full emptiness reminiscent of the darkness of the womb. Osho, a contemporary, spiritual teacher says 'To create nothingness in you is the goal of meditation, but it has nothing to do with the negative idea. If it is negative it is like death, darkness. But this is full, abundantly full.'

Amidst our culture of doing, I have come to realize that depression is about being... about enduring, about suffering meaning. Within this matrix of loss and disintegration emerges a new foundation within whose soils germinate seeds of wisdom; their harvest can be a deepening spirituality.

A lot of illness, regardless of what organ or bodily system it affects, can be reoccurring and cyclical. There are remissions which may last months, even years, followed by subsequent debilitating periods of dis-ease which may become more progressive as time goes by. Again, our culture of fixing and curing illness undermines the potential of these periods of being, so that we long for health in order to feel normal. And by this I am not advocating that illness, dis-ease and sickness should be revered and not treated, but valued while it is in residence in our lives. Although we may not feel we have invited it, "dis-ease is our soul's guest" as Jungian therapist, Thomas Moore, so cogently expresses it, and therefore has a valid place in our life development.

Depression, the shadow side of our doing culture, because of its relative invisibility, carries the most shame and least understanding and empathy as a dis-ease next to AIDS. Because all of us, if we are honest, have been depressed at some point in our life, often our outlook can be judgmental, rather than empathic. If we feel we should 'snap out of it' then we expect others to do the same. We might even, covertly, look upon those who fail to do so as weak and inadequate. This outlook, although seemingly personal in nature, is shaped by the culture of shame that has been built around depression.

Although depressive episodes in response to loss and difficulty are a natural reaction, depression that is recurrent and interferes with normal functioning of everyday life needs to be taken seriously as it is potentially life threatening. Although the sufferer may find it hard to seek help when his/her energy levels are so low, it is important that medical help is sought, both for diagnoses and a means of support, whether this comes through medication or therapeutic counseling. Like heart disease, serious depression can be life threatening in that the depressive is often plagued by suicidal thoughts which may be acted out. As I illustrate later in my section, *Tools on the Journey* (Chapter 6), there is ample medical evidence today that links depression with heart disease, diabetes and cancer. As Psychiatrist, Peter Kramer, and author of the bestselling book, *Listening to Prozac*, writes 'Depression affects multiple organs....The disruptions to prefrontal cortex, hippocampus, adrenals, bones, glands, heart, and blood – these constitute a particular disorder.'

On a personal level, I fought medication and therapy for a number of years, limping along with an assortment of alternative medicines which worked marginally well, if at all. Looking back, I held onto the fact that my spiritual awareness and background should be all that I needed. Really, this masked a covert spiritual pride that somehow I was exempt from the same sort of depression as 'other' people. It was only when I had enough humility to accept that the medical profession was held within the same healing field as alternative medicine practitioners, that I began to accept the medicine that greatly alleviated my mental and emotional torture.

It took much longer to realize that my depressive episodes were worsening and that I was 'stuck' with this dis-ease for life. Even longer to realize, and six years of psychotherapy and training in psychosynthesis psychology, that this depression, which had greatly hindered my ability to hold down a career or plan too far ahead, *was my spiritual journey!* Up until that point I had tried to ignore it, fix it and transform it, but it was here to stay, either waiting in the wings or taking up center stage.

A subsequent spell in a psychiatric unit amplified the severity of my condition, though I have to say that the experience itself was a very healing one and played a transformative part in my development, as well as being crucial to my understanding and acceptance of depression. Today's medications and therapies, although very effective in alleviating the anguish of depressive illness, such as sleeplessness, anxiety, suicidal thoughts, like all medications have their shortcomings. This mainly manifests in the duration of efficacy. A medication may work very effectively for a while but then, as the bodily system acclimatizes to the treatment, the medicine becomes less effective and a new medicine has to be introduced which can take a few agonizing weeks to become effective. Exceptions abound where people have been helped enormously with a drug for many years and lived a near to normal life, yet there are sufferers who have found no relief in medication and have had to resort to other treatments such as Electro-Convulsive Therapy (ECT). Again, although sounding antiquated and barbaric, this is no different to administering shock treatment to the heart in cardiac arrest, except that it is applied to the brain instead.

Although mild depression exists along the same continuum as moderate and major depression, it may or may not progress to the more extreme category. Depressive episodes that begin in the teens have a tendency to recur if no treatment is available. If there is a history of depressive episodes in the family and mental breakdown, there is very likely to be a fifty percent hereditary factor present. This may offer a predetermined influence, but the way one approaches the problem is not pre-destined. The importance and learning is not so much in *what* we have to cope with in life, but *how* we deal with the difficulty. In a sense, because technology has accelerated ahead at breakneck speed, we need to simultaneously deepen our spiritual understanding in order to keep abreast with these changes.

In order to define depression farther in this work, I want

mainly to address moderate to major depression, bipolar disorder, and seasonal affective disorder.

Moderate to Major Depression

The distinctions between moderate and major depression can be largely defined as the level and breadth of intensity and duration of mood together with how this impacts on the physical body. Moderate depression may last only a few days or weeks and despite being depleted of energy, one can still carry on a normal life. The point at which depression becomes debilitating, or even life threatening, is where moderate becomes major depression. Depressive symptoms so eclipse a person's life that they can no longer live it in a comfortable way.

Andrew Solomon, author of *The Noonday Demon*, describes major depression as 'a birth and a death'. He equates the birth with the depression which, like a vine, takes possession of the oak tree, gradually leaching it of all life. This is the gradual death because depression creeps up insidiously on you, taking hold of your thoughts and gradually distorting them, turning them inward. Often, like the aura that precedes an epileptic fit in the form of a recognizable smell, depression makes its presence known some time before it takes up residence in the soul. It is like that day in the middle of August where the scent in the air changes, becoming sharper, richer and earthier. We lift our faces to the wind and know that the fall is approaching. We acknowledge it, shiver, and know that summer is slipping inexorably away. The season is changing, but then summer is back again. Several days might pass, and then we experience that sharpness again, notice the few scattering leaves and know that we have passed into the penumbra of the fall.

Little signs make themselves known as time goes by, as the summer dances alongside the approaching fall, and we pass through a chequer board of fall and summer. All change, although we may be blind to it, begins to announce its arrival from the wings long in advance.

Martha Manning, a psychologist and sufferer of major depression, writes compellingly about this slow eclipsing of her everyday life before a depressive episode:

> I'm fading, slipping into the arms of a depression that has been lurking but that I've been able to shake off somehow. ...I'm falling farther and farther behind, slowing down. I know this territory. I withdraw from other people as much as possible, not wanting to impose myself on them and also not be embarrassed by myself, for myself. Sleep is a stranger. My optimism about the future is gone. And all I can do is cry and pray, God, please don't let me go back to that place where death looks more beautiful than life, where putting one foot in front of the other, is a day's work, where combing my hair and getting dressed seem an unfamiliar process and interactions with people deserve academy Awards for acting. I'm afraid I won't make it back this time.

Amidst this approaching depression there is a sense of powerlessness and frustration that may erupt in anger, tears, even self harm. The danger period, where suicidal tendencies may be strongest, lie within this liminal, 'between and betwixt', stage of the rocking foundations of everyday life and the descent into the depths. After descent, there is a sense of imprisonment where self-will is diminished. Major depression is harrowing in that the harder we try to fight its rigorous onslaught, the stronger it appears to become. Like a butterfly caught in a web, we fight a losing battle to free ourselves from the deceptively strong silken threads.

Major depression tends to last for several months, on average six months which, interestingly, corresponds to the period Demeter's daughter Persephone was imprisoned in the Underworld. I explore this cycle of rupturing foundations, descent, imprisonment, transformation and emergence in my chapter, *Persephone and the Underworld* (Chapter 5).

Prescribed medication during this period may alleviate sleeplessness and restore the appetite as well as mitigating some of the pain so one is able to function marginally in the world. A good therapist can offer the empathy and support which is needed. Partners and loved ones sadly often bear the anguish of feeling unable to alleviate the pain or find a solution. To watch a loved one suffer and experience their powerlessness beside our own is immensely frustrating. To hold hope when our loved one's last vestige has long been extinguished seems impossible. It is as if we are immured in an impossible situation where we can easily end up resenting each other, rather than the illness.

There may be a year or so between episodes, but this varies from person to person. Basically, major depression tends to leave the individual vulnerable to stress which can trigger off further full-blown episodes. Like all illness, depression leaves its imprint on the life, creating disruptions in career, broken marriages, and estranged family members. I have come into contact with many young people who have had to drop out of university because of episodes and others who have found it impossible to share their life with a partner. More often than not, people with alcohol or addiction problems have a history of mental illness and depression. I have come across many patients in hospital who are in the end stages of alcoholic liver disease who have used alcohol to cope with deep depression. Depression that may have been occluded by the addiction, overlooked or not even recognized. Many have lost their jobs, their families, and their self esteem.

Many homeless people emerge from a history of depression which has prevented sustainability of employment. It is so easy to drop out of the holding system of everyday life in the absence of family and friends and even easier to choose a way of escaping the hell of deepening depression through drugs. Career changes, relationship hopping and moving location may offer temporary relief, but not for long. Furthermore, many employers steer clear of employing people who have a history of depression, understandably because of the impact this will have on the company in lost working hours.

There are still other people who may struggle on in their working lives, following careers in high powered jobs amidst depressive episodes. Close work colleagues may be aware of their struggle and make allowances for them in their dark periods. Many people who suffer from severe depression are hardworking, conscientious and highly skilled – and most of all, as Martha Manning intimates, 'good actors'!

Sometimes a clear distinction can be made between moderate and major depression from the degree of psychosis that may be evident. Psychosis is not only the byproduct of delusional thinking and hallucinations, but when one's sense of reality breaks down to such a degree that one loses ones sense of 'I'. Usually, in any experience, there is an observing component to the self. Despite the relative physical or mental discomfort of the situation, the individual is able to know that this discomfort is not *all* of him. In essence, he is in touch with his inner centre. This allows one to possess a certain amount of detachment from the debilitating experience. Basically, there is a residual deep knowing amidst the chaos that 'this too shall pass.' In psychoses this mediating centre and sense of 'I' is lost or, rather, overwhelmed by the unconscious. The wall of psychic defense is broken down, and the tide of the unconscious rushes in. One is overcome and needs medical intervention of some kind.

If we are to be honest with ourselves, we are all mildly neurotic, mildly paranoid and psychotic at times! We all possess pockets of neuroses and mood disorders, but our observing 'I' maintains the homeostasis between our inner world and outer world reality.

Seasonal Affective Disorder

Although most depression is governed by cyclical factors, there is a type of depression, seasonally affective disorder (commonly referred to as SAD) that visits many of us in the less temperate latitude each fall. Most of us feel a little low and depleted after basking in the sunlight for the summer months, when the days become shorter and the leaves begin to turn color. The seasonal nature of life mirrors an identical inner process as we witness signs of this in the migration of swallows and swifts back to Africa at the end of August. We might experience a sinking feeling, an inner restlessness that the summer is over with a sense that we should change our direction in life and do something different. It is a deeply instinctive force that has guided migratory paths globally for hundreds of years. Is it so unusual that we, who are intrinsically linked with nature and the past, should be influenced by the same instincts that held our nomadic ancestors to a greater or lesser degree? We are effectively, like nature, beginning to close down; the sap has descended to the ground and animals around us are preparing for hibernation or storing up resources for the lean winter months ahead.

Yet, it seems, the culture we live in no longer has space for the seasonal preparations of our ancestors. We have lost touch with the equinoxes and solstices and so it seems the deep impulses for birth and death, hibernation and exploration, take us by surprise and make us feel less than normal.

The symptoms of SAD can be mild to severe and life threatening. As with most depressive disorders, there is a slowing down of physical and mental activity accompanied by a need to sleep. This is different to other depressive illnesses where there is a marked problem with going to sleep or staying asleep. In most cases of SAD the appetite is increased with a longing for carbohydrate foods and chocolate which boost the serotonin levels that are depleted by the diminished daylight hours. The descent into depression can last anything from September to

May or, in more moderate cases, appear after Christmas and become reduced in the spring. What many sufferers of SAD find helpful is the daily intervention of light therapy. This is administered through a light box with a full spectrum light source, at least 2500 lux, which is five times brighter than a well-lit office. A bright spring day would produce 10,000 lux and obviously light boxes that offer this amount of lux work faster and may require only 20 minutes exposure as opposed to 45 minutes for the 2500 lux ones.

As SAD is triggered by a 'biochemical imbalance in the hypothalamus' in response to the diminishing daylight hours, there is also evidence that light affects the pineal gland, a small pea-sized gland in the centre of the brain. Functioning like a biological clock, it orchestrates the pace of the daily circadian rhythms. Among other hormones, the pineal plays an important part in the secretion of melatonin, which implements the ability to sleep and increases serotonin levels in the brain. When the eyes are exposed to light, they create nerve impulses which travel directly to the pineal gland. In this sense, the body's inner clock runs on light or solar power. Interestingly, in mystical tradition, the pineal gland has always been referred to as the third eye.

Of course there is nothing to compare with exposure to natural daylight in the open air, and light therapy can be easily incorporated by a daily walk in half an hour's sunshine. If depression is a dreaded seasonal event and if finances permit, holidays can be taken in the winter sun, not necessarily in warmer climes, but also in Scandinavia in February and March when the days are getting longer, or winter skiing areas where sun on the snow intensifies the brilliance of the light. Generally, there is a sense of slow steady emergence with the lengthening spring days, but for some this immersion in darkness may drag on until May. If untreated, this descent may last for increasingly longer periods each year and become more critical as time goes by. This is mainly due to hippocampal shrinkage in the brain and the damage to the prefrontal cortex if major depressive episodes are left untreated. This only serves to reinforce the importance of getting treatment swiftly.

Again, the liminal period between descent in the fall and ascent in the spring is critical. Doctors and psychiatrists know that the most critical time in treatment for depression is not when the sufferer is at their worst, devoid of feeling; it is during that period when they are getting better, feelings are beginning to return, thoughts are flowing again and the mood fluctuations between feeling suicidal and feeling well are 'cycling' rapidly. As this often happens during medical intervention, resources need to be more widely available to monitor the progress of each patient. Feeling suicidal can be the return of feelings that were dead before. Becoming better can be as hazardous as becoming ill. Too often the medication that triggers the return of feelings is blamed, rather than promoting any understanding of this critical period during the healing crisis. Having experienced this very real crisis myself on a number of occasions, both through a natural emergence from seasonal depression as well as a pharmacological one, I am only too aware of the lack of insight and understanding about this. And here the maxim, 'the darkest hour is always before the dawn', can be helpful to both healer and patient. In fact, this phrase was enough to turn the corner for one of my colleagues.

Bipolar Disorder

Again, like SAD, bipolar disorder (otherwise known as manic depression) is highly seasonal in nature. This is a major depressive disorder where mood swings can oscillate between periods of euphoria, relative normality and suicidal depression. Psychiatrist, Kay Redfield Jamieson, who suffers from bipolar disorder herself, writes 'The rhythms and cycles of manic depressive illness, a singularly cyclic disease, are strikingly similar to those of the natural world.'

Bipolar disorder has a strong genetic determination of 80 percent. Its onset tends to be earlier than other depressive conditions, the average being around 21 years old. Episodes of euphoria and depression may last anything from a few days to a few months. There are two subsets of bipolar disorder, known as type 1 (hypermania) and type 2 (hypomania). Basically, type 1 is the more manic version which often requires hospitalization. Type 2 is less manic, presenting itself as mildly euphoric and with greater emphasis on the depressive cycle.

In type 1, the most effective treatments for bipolar disorder are mood stabilizers like carbemazepine or lithium, which is a form of sodium. The interesting thing here is when British actor, Stephen Fry, and other bipolar sufferers were asked how they would feel if their illness was taken away, the majority, including Fry, would prefer not to be without it. The promise of the highs seems to far outweigh the impotence of the lows. One man, who believed that he was in touch with angels during his manic phases, believed that the veil gets lifted when entering this 'psychotic' world and one is able to see things in a different way. He firmly stated 'If you walked with angels all the pain and suffering is worthwhile.'

Although this richly illustrates the spiritual aspect held within the illness, I have to say that not all people suffering from bipolar will experience this. Some individuals can experience prolonged periods of normality, interspersed with an episode of being hypermanic or descending to the depths, there are many where periods of normality are few and far between. At the mercy of protracted periods of being too clinically depressed or loquaciously exuberant to function in normal everyday life, medication can be life saving. Of course there are milder forms of manic depression, but I have come across few manic depressives who have not had their life scarred by this illness. Even when people seem to have their illness under control, mostly with the aid of medication, their respite from the extremes cannot be taken for granted. A little more stress than usual or a transition from one seasonal cycle to another can trigger off an episode which might be intense enough to require hospitalization for their own safety.

I have a friend, a gifted music teacher, who has suffered from it for most of her life and despite medication and withdrawing from too much stress she experiences acute difficulty managing to maintain equilibrium. The unfortunate thing with bipolar, like most 'dis-eases', is that it tends to progress with age. And in manic depressive disorder, as I was told by a very good psychiatrist of mine, one tends to polarize to either the manic or depressed phase which becomes more and more extreme as the neuronal pathways begin to atrophy. In the case of Sheelagh, she often finds that after several months of feeling low, she is beginning to feel better, even well. But then this, in a matter of days, can proceed to a 'better than well' feeling. She is exuberant, talkative, and full of ideas with tremendous energy to implement them. After knowing how low she has been, it is wonderful to see her happy and enjoying life. But, even as she admits, there is a fine line between feeling very well and tipping the balance to mania. She will convince herself and me that she is just happy and feeling well again. "And you know something, Steph," she says "God is back... I just feel a beautiful presence with me and I know everything is going to be all right."

I am always happy for her, though I know how tenuous this sense of wellbeing can be. But then she notices she needs less and less sleep, perhaps no more than two hours a night, then she is out walking the dog, shopping and everything is 'wonderful'. She admits to me that she is feeling high but thinks she can cope with it, hiding it from the community psychiatric nurse who visits. But then she can no longer hide it; she is taking the car out, driving about in her pajamas and the community psychiatric nurse, who is in touch with her psychiatrist, suggests she is becoming manic... Not wanting to get admitted to hospital again, she reluctantly accepts the Largactil and within twenty four hours is a shadow of herself. And I feel for her as I watch her slow labored movements where everything is an effort and her eyes are dull and clouded and the light in her eyes merely a ghost that has long departed. I know that it will be a few days before she begins to crawl up from rock bottom again as the medication tapers off and she finds herself in the residual low period, when she feels dead inside. What saddens me is that she has lost that sense of connection with the divine again.

I know that the feeling of spiritual connection which, creatively, I experienced as a song within me, where I felt I was in touch with something greater than myself, could be as addictive as the drugs people use to reach euphoric states in their longing for union with that same force. The manic depressive, who cannot help but experience the pull to the heights, is a living metaphor for the legendary Icarus' flight to the sun that melts his great waxen wings and drops like a stone into the ocean to drown in the sea of the unconscious. Not everyone who experiences the heights translates their experience into contact with the transpersonal; instead they will believe it to be themselves. On the personality level they believe *they* are the light and have messianic experiences. The energies of the Self are hard to contain because they are so powerful and fulfill that deep longing that many of us have for spiritual connection.

I once met someone in a bipolar organization, of which I was a member, who used to edit the newsletter. I was sitting in the car and he said jokingly: "Whenever I think I'm God, Betty, my wife reminds me that I need to go up on my medication!"

If most depressive illness portrays a grim wilderness and an absence of spiritual connection, bipolar disorder, often during its hypomanic phase, reveals the opposite of this. Virginia Woolf, who suffered from bipolar illness, writes about this in *A Room of One's Own*.

'The beauty of the World has two edges, one of laughter, one of anguish, cutting the heart asunder,' Jamison, a psychiatrist and a sufferer of bipolar disorder, writes. She herself researched the link with bipolar disorder and the creative temperament within the life of artists, writers and poets and explores both mania and hypomania extensively in her book, *Touched with Fire*.

Bipolar disorder is believed to be a hereditary illness where the sufferer experiences cyclical phases of heightened emotions (that are often euphoric in nature) and increased mental ability in the form of inspiration. The manic phase is accompanied by intense energy and grandiosity with the alternating phase of enervation, deep melancholia and mental sluggishness. These cycles are recurrent and tend to fall into step with the seasons; moving from winter deadness to exuberance within the summer months. During the manic phase there is a sense of connectivity with all life. John Ruskin writes 'I am almost sick and giddy with the quantity of things in my head – trains of thought beginning and branching to infinity...' And poet, Theodore Roethke, expresses 'Suddenly I knew how it felt to be a tree, a blade of grass...' Socrates went on to refer to this mania as 'a divine madness' which he described as being a gift from God.

Amidst this euphoric phase, floodgates of inspiration are thrown open and the subject is capable of a vast output of creativity which, if harnessed and channeled in a productive way, can be deeply fulfilling to one's professional life. In fact, it is the ability to work with this condition by grounding it in a creative way which becomes the key to integrating these energies flooding in from the Self. Others, who are not as fortunate to find an outlet for them, may attribute these energies to the personality and express a spirited sense of grandiosity. Psychiatrist and founder of Psychosynthesis, Roberto Assagioli, warns against this when the ego is not strong enough to assimilate the energies of the Self and the experience inflates the personality and feeds the narcissistic impulses. This is why bipolar people suffering from hypermania can seem full of themselves and unable to empathize with the feelings of anyone else they come into contact with.

Dark Night of the Soul and Creative Depression

I want to briefly include here what is known as 'Dark Night of the Soul' after St John of the Cross. This is a more mystical type of depression, which I cover extensively later on in the book. Particularly, I feel that the 'Dark Night of the Senses,' which is the initial phase of the 'Dark Night of the Soul', where there is an eclipsing of the value we derive from objects and sensual experience, has importance today. This eclipse sends the spiritually impoverished individual on the quest for soul-making.

In the face of creative depression many of us are unfamiliar with the value of frustration and stand-still which, on another level, are valuable ground for developing insight and inspiration (see Chapter 14). We do not know what to do with creative darkness and cannot see that it is a crucial element in a much larger process. By not following periods of creative darkness through, we miss the vital insight that is waiting for us to discover.

Loss of Spiritual Connection

Alongside the crippling loss of purpose and meaning in depressive illness, perhaps the most isolating and excruciatingly painful condition for the sufferer is the loss of spiritual connection. Depression, by its very nature, is an illness of isolation. For those who have a strong spiritual context for their life, this alienation from God is even more crippling than alienation from family and friends. A colleague of mine, who, when he was well, maintained a regular spiritual practice through meditation and prayer, found that he could do neither any more. At the very least he felt deserted by God, and at the most punished for a crime he didn't commit. This is expressed so well by the late American poet, Jane Kenyon's, verses who, herself, suffered from depression:

With the wonder
and bitterness of someone pardoned
for a crime she did not commit
I come back to marriage and friends,
to pink fringed hollyhocks; come back
to my desk, books, and chair.

Often people who suffer from depressive illness develop or have an inherent sense of spirituality. Their spiritual life gives content and meaning to their life journey. As Paul Watson, evolutionary biologist, suggests:

Within the next 50-200 years, it doesn't really matter, the pharmaceutical industry is going to have to have our neuro-chemistry down to the point where they will be able to save us from having any adverse internal experience, no matter how our life is actually going... Before we start turning off all these unpleasant experiences, we need to know what these unpleasant experiences are for.

And the question I want to carry with me through this work is: What does depression serve? Hopefully, we can move nearer to aligning with the answer hidden in the question as this work continues to unfold.

Chapter 3

Depression as a Spiritual Journey

A hero ventures forth from the world of the common day into a region
of supernatural wonder. Fabulous forces are there encountered and a
decisive victory is won. The hero comes back from this mysterious
adventure with the power to bestow boons on his fellow man.
Joseph Campbell, The Hero with a Thousand Faces

From the moment we emerge into the world we are participating in a journey. Not just an isolated journey, but one interwoven with many other journeys which all network together to form an individual life history. Semantically, we refer to this as a biography. We know from reading biographies that, although the person may have died, they come alive again as we divine the meaning of the words and trace the connections to the people, places and events enfolded in the story as it unfolds. We can use a single tree in a forest as a metaphor for this; although an individual, with its own unique pattern of growth and development, it still has living connections with the forest it is a part of.

The journey we make before we even reach kindergarten or can begin to articulate our story, begins in the womb. Birth opens up another journey which brings us in close proximity with parents or carers who guide and foster our development and hold the boundaries by keeping us safe from danger. Within this matrix we learn to walk, articulate our needs and live the journey that unfolds before us. I want to suggest that each journey follows three main sequences:

- The Beginning: The Call to Adventure
- The Middle: Trials and Tribulations
- The Return

Most stories have a beginning, middle and an end, and you will notice that I do not use the word 'end' here to describe the third sequence because it is a term endemic in our culture where curves and circles and the natural cyclical courses of events are erased. Although there is completion there is never an end. T.S Elliot refers obliquely to this when opening his poem, *The Four Quartets*: 'In my beginning is my end,' and then closes it with the lines: 'In my end is my beginning.' *End and beginning are interchangeable.*

Embarking on any journey that takes us away from the safety of home and the known is an adventure; we want to learn to ride a bike, go camping or swimming; we want to grow up, study, take time out and travel or train for a new career, start a new job and develop new skills – these are all calls to adventure. Here, in the realm of the spirit, nothing is ordinary and mundane.

I would suggest that falling in love is probably one of the most awesome, terrifying, exhilarating adventures we can embark on. Journeys which open our heart hold the deepest impressions because love is the alchemical substance that transforms the psyche and the individual life. Falling in love may not be with a person, but can as readily be a place, a vocation, or a deep mission in life to transform, heal or regenerate a condition. Falling in love immediately activates a sense of purpose, meaning and values. Without this vital activation of the heart our lives fall short of what they can be and our sense of inner impoverishment inevitably takes us on the journey of dis-ease, because the heart needs to open. This dis-ease can take the form of depression, mental and emotional instability, bodily and relationship breakdown. The journey of dis-ease and impoverishment is one of trial and tribulation and is no less important than any other journey because, ultimately, it is one of soul-making where the heart may begin to open.

It is as if the passage to change and transformation is the journey's intent whether we want this or not. There is no time limit on this. In the realm of the spirit, time is inconsequential. Every journey involves process; however, if the process is interrupted in any way, the end result is compromised. But something will be gained from this as nothing is truly lost; it is just transformed. However, the so called 'aborted' journey can fast track us onto another journey if we allow it to. And here we enter the realm of soul-making where new meaning and insight is available.

If the initiate is up for the trials of the path he will create a 'Vision Quest'. In Amerindian lore this was where a young pubescent boy would enter a trance (an altered state of being) in order to find his next clue. This vision quest was a passage through a threshold from the known and mundane world to the unknown and soul world. Combating demands within himself, in the form of earlier historical injunctions and social norms, the initiate lays himself open to the teaching that confronts him and in this way undergoes initiation. This is laid out fully in the *Journey of Persephone to the Underworld* (see Chapter 5), which we will explore shortly. Anything that is born or created emerges through the public domain, the world. However, we don't give birth just for our own sake. It is as if every 'hero' we bring into the world, be it a child or creative project, exists to serve the whole. Whether we like it or not, what is created has its own journey, however much we may want to control and shape that biography. The best we can do is facilitate its passage.

The nature of a journey may to be simply to *experience*, not necessarily to reach a conclusion which is hard to comprehend through the lens of our 'go getting' culture where every step is polarized to product, result and success.

In an age and culture where life processes were valued for what they were rather than what they weren't, there were 'rites of passage' to enable pubescent young men and women to reach adulthood. The facilitators and shamans in this had passed through the same process themselves and knew the territory well. Through our Westernized and so called 'civilized eyes' the initiate suffered pain and deprivation. Such practices were later deemed as barbaric and fell under the negative designation of magic and witchcraft. Yet, in sharp contrast, our own practices in negotiating the transition from childhood to adulthood may seem to an outsider not only barbaric and uncivilized but without any meaning or value. As Saturday nights in Western society collapse into drunken orgies where children end up in Accident and Emergency (A&E) with drug abuse, suicide attempts and knife wounds, there seems to be little gained from this regular assault on the senses.

Yet, by returning to the truth 'nothing is lost, no journey is a failure', we are invited to look at it in another way. Everything that happens externally is a mirror for what is happening intrapsychically. Our children are only reflecting the culture they are expected to participate in where meaning, purpose, and value seem to be sacrificed for an essentially materialistic society. It is, after all, to this 'holy cow' that we pay homage. Our young are merely reflecting back our loss of soul.

According to Jay Griffiths, writer for *Resurgence* and author of *Wild, an Elemental Journey*, this spiritual dis-ease is not just confined to the West. Soul unrest among the young extends to areas as remote as the deserts of central Australia, the ghettos of Southern Africa and the Arctic. The underlying cause of this unrest is 'being outside nature'. The land heals, the wise people tell us, particularly those of the Inuit community. This is why these programs which take young people out in the wilderness are becoming so popular and successful. These are journeys into wild nature which calm the imprisoned spirit in young people. Without this contact with elders and wise people who can guide the young soul into purpose, meaning and values, the wild and untamed energy inside a young person can turn against itself, becoming violent and regressing into gangland warfare. It is as if discovering the spirit in the wild places speaks to the trapped spirit within and allows it to breathe and be, so that the young people can return to their own land and call out the spirit there. The land, its ecology and people are inextricably bound with spirit. Historically, we can see where Western material values have gained a hold on isolated communities; values and purpose have plummeted into alcoholism, self-harm and drug culture. When we take away a people's purpose, we take away their life. This has happened to the Aborigine, the Amerindian and many of the Amazonian people where their forest and land have been polluted by Western greed and materialism.

All journeys are essentially inner ones because what is experienced externally passes into the domain of soul-making. But we may choose to become unconscious to this. By our choice and actions we define who we are and who we are not.

Because, so much worldly emphasis has been placed on the outer discernable journey of prestige and success, we therefore become unconscious to anything which threatens these values. And yet, it seems that many people are looking for reconnection with the sacred. Perhaps we are looking for a respite from the deep emptiness inside us from all the glittering temptations pouring through the lens of the media in glossy magazines and sensually laden TV commercials. One of the top searches on the internet is for holidays (holy days). On one level we want to run away from our mundane everyday life, on another level we are longing to engage in adventure. Some of us opt for 'adventure holidays' but these 'adventures' are monitored and controlled with safety mechanisms embedded in the template. We take out insurance to shield us from calamity, and the trekking or boating trails we follow are carefully worked out beforehand. In short, we fight shy of anything that has a hidden edge of trial and tribulation, that second stage of the journey. In reality, it is not the workplace we are running away from – it is the soul: the part of us that is ever struggling to find a voice through our symptoms and neuroses.

But one in five of us are going through an inner journey, whether we admit it to ourselves or not in the form of depression which is the subject of this book... If depression is so common, in that people from every walk of life in the Western world are engaged in it, why are we running away from it? Depression takes us deep into the domain of the soul, and the trials and tribulations we suffer in order to serve soul-making are true engagement in the spiritual journey.

In the next chapter I want to look at the role of making meaning out of our suffering along with the distinctions in suffering on the level of body/personality, soul and spirit.

Chapter 4

The Meaning of Suffering

Why? Why me? Is often the immediate response to suffering. Looking for meaning comes later when the anger and anguish have bared the 'soulscape' within.

I would suggest that there is an intimate connection between soul-making and suffering. It is through suffering that we enter into relationship with the world of soul and the potential richness of its wisdom. This can be illustrated through the work of those men and women in history who underwent great physical, mental and emotional deprivation and were brought in touch with a source of rich nourishment that sustained them through their inner internment. It is not surprising that this contact with this source became known as 'the imprisoned splendor', because it was in a state of imprisonment, either covert or overt, that this splendor became realized. We can look at the lives of Dante (whose imprisonment birthed *The Divine Comedy*), John Bunyan (who produced *Pilgrim's Progress*) and Oscar Wilde (who wrote *De Profundis*) and see how imprisonment can be a living and working metaphor for 'soul- making'. The expression the poet John Keats used to describe the world with all its pain and trouble was literally, *The Vale of Soul-making*.

'Where there is sorrow there is holy ground,' Wilde wrote. Later, he added 'It is tragic how few people ever possess their souls before they die.' As Wilde portrays in his seminal and reflective work, written during his imprisonment in Reading Goal, *De Profundis*,

Life without soul is a shallow empty one without meaning. Life without meaning is one that cannot survive long when faced with difficulty and disaster as it is without direction or roots which would lend the necessary strength required to sustain us through spiritual and emotional aridity.

Psychiatrist, Viktor Frankyl, discovered this when he endured years of torture and abuse in a Nazi death camp. He found that prisoners' capacity to endure suffering was increased when they were able to see meaning in their suffering. This meaning had to correspond with internal values rather than worldly ones that are transitory in nature, like prestige and success. He believed that 'suffering ceases to be suffering at the moment it finds a meaning, such as the meaning of sacrifice.'

While suffering is resisted, it is debilitating and humiliating. By finding meaning in it, either through identifying with a cause or purpose, the relationship with pain is transmuted. Pain is no longer an 'it' visiting its unwelcome attention upon the sufferer; it is a quality that unlocks the 'imprisoned splendor' in the one who suffers. Suffering instead ensouls the suffering 'I', helping to transform the unbearable into the bearable. The personality which, before, sought to defend itself against suffering, surrenders to it instead and humiliation gives way to humility.

In a culture that denigrates and cuts off from suffering under its guises of loss, failure and illness and therefore exiling the soul from everyday language and contact, it is no wonder that depressive illness is rampant. We comfort ourselves with pension and insurance schemes that maintain our security needs. In fact, our lifestyle is a defense against suffering in any form. But in our efforts to deny the soul a voice, we create an underground culture of nihilism, lived out by our disillusioned young in drug abuse and petty crimes.

Just as suffering is intimately bound to the soul, so is pleasure the antithesis of suffering. Yet, in Oscar Wilde's admission that he spent the earlier part of his life in the pursuit of pleasure, which he believed took him to the depths of depravity, it was through this very avoidance that led him full circle to the feet of his soul. He admitted he had lived life fully, to know life fully. Like the prodigal son who sought to fully incarnate into the world through squandering everything he had, he had suffered nemesis which had finally led him back to his Father, the Spirit, or the Self.

The Three Levels of Suffering

We suffer through three distinct levels of being, all of which most of us will recognize:

Personality/body
Soul
Spirit

On the personality level, we endeavor to identify our condition through finding a therapist, psychiatrist or doctor. We want our suffering to go away and we try to fix it, exorcize and cauterize it from our being. At this point we are not preoccupied by meaning or content, only by getting rid of discomfort. This stage is principally about history, about fixing the aberration.

The suffering soul is led to find meaning and purpose in its condition by experience in matter. This leads him on the journey of finding a cure for his malady and learning all that can be found about his condition. But as cures fail in the form of medications or therapies which no longer work, he/she becomes angry. He/she asks why. Why has this happened to me? What have I done to deserve this? The soul experiences alienation from Spirit and longs for release from that which keeps him separate from that union – namely the suffering. But gradually the suffering wears away the anger and it is as if the soul opens to the pain and he/she realizes that he/she is part of something greater. Knowing this brings a sense of relief and release, and it is here at this critical juncture that he/she realizes he/she is Spirit in matter that suffers or bears meaning. There may be a sense of inner cruci-fixion in this.

In suffering meaning on the level of spirit, the suffering has nothing to do with history; it just 'is' and this is the bond that links all life together. But this sort of acceptance is not the same as resignation and apathy that can take place on the level of the personality and soul.

Between the level of soul and spirit there may be much delib-eration, when meaning-making can become a manic defense against entering the next level – that of the spirit. Where depression may be understood to manifest through genetic constellations within the ancestral lineage and may respond to some sort of medication or treatment, there is also the necessary loss of that perspective. Medication, psychotherapy, knowledge and understanding cannot fix the malady. Like the Fisher King's wound in Arthurian legend that never heals, depression cannot be eradicated completely. It is within the gradual dissolution of this 'cure-it' mindset that another level of meaning is sought. And the archetypal question is asked: If nothing can heal this wound, then what does it serve?

Similarly, David Karp, Professor of Sociology, writes about the three stages of adaptation when he describes the movement from realizing one has a depressive illness, to experimenting with different medications and therapies in an effort to treat it. Finally, there is a movement to a deeper level of acceptance. This often follows a period of disillusionment, when one realizes that despite efforts to fix the condition, depressive illness still predominates. At this level, meaning is no longer sought in an effort to assuage the wound and understand its purpose. One suffers meaning and this may be actualized by becoming a guide or therapist to others who suffer with the same condition. Karp writes 'Once individuals realize that medical treatment is unlikely to fix their problem, their thinking moves away from the medical language of cure and toward the *spiritual* language of transformation.'

Since depression is an illness where lack of connection and social isolation are experienced keenly, as in all illnesses that open up ground to the soul, it also opens the heart to compassion. The Arthurian Fisher King's wound that will not heal becomes, instead, a sensitive lens through which one experiences the collective wound of the world. Supporting this, Thomas Moore writes 'Accepting that we are wounded, we enter life differently than if our only concern is to overcome the wound.'

As the Dalai Lama, in his discourses, urges us to have compassion for each other, the very nature of depression urges us to care and listen to our wound and develop a 'right relationship' with our source of suffering. In developing a meaningful relationship with our own suffering we are able to receive the suffering of others. In this, we become Chiron, the wounded healer, whose gift is borne of his own suffering.

Although depression, like many illnesses, may present itself in individual cases, it is also a symptom of a collective problem. Karp writes 'The Iroquois Indians believed that when any single person suffered it reflected the suffering of nature, of the whole world, in fact.' All suffering leads back to the soul. In this sense, it is possible to see that suffering through depression is an initiatory journey, one that Wilde asserts in *De Profundis* 'remarries us to God'.

Suffering through the Lens of the Major Religions

As suffering brings us intimately in touch with the soul and its spiritual significance in our lives, it is worth dipping into the five major world religions and seeing how they each interpret the role of suffering in the human life. Both Islam and Christianity talk about the 'mystery' of suffering and that with our finite minds we may never know God or Allah's will. In short, suffering creates meaning and opens the heart to divine love.

Buddhism's first two noble truths purport that all life is suffering and is caused by attachment to worldly things. In fact, Buddha was known to have asked a woman who complained of the difficulties placed in her own life, to find someone who didn't suffer. After knocking on all the doors of the community where she lived, she returned empty handed. Buddhism's fundamental model of redemption from the sin of past actions is lived out through the law of karma. This karmic thread works its way through the individual cycles of reincarnation, but the Buddhist philosophy warns us to be careful of placing judgment on others as we cannot know whether the person or group of people suffering are working out personal or collective karma. Also karma may be taken on voluntarily as an act of service for humanity and can be instrumental in leading all those involved, such as relatives and friends, into the deeper mysteries of life. The grain of sand in the oyster that becomes a priceless pearl is an excellent metaphor for the meaning of suffering and suffering meaning.

Christianity holds the 'unjustified suffering of the innocent' at the heart of its teaching, often referring to this in the metaphor of the 'sacrificial lamb'. According to St Paul, Christians should rejoice in suffering because it prioritizes endurance. Some Christians see natural disaster as God inflicting punishment on a population. Fourth century Saint Augustine said 'God would not allow any evil to exist unless out of it he could draw a greater good.'

Pope John Paul II wrote about the distinction between physical and moral suffering, the latter of which was of a spiritual nature. He referred to this as 'pain of the soul'. He believed that this form of suffering is the most resistant and unreachable by therapy. In the context of this book, depressive illness is most often a 'soul suffering' which is exacerbated not just by the alienation from ordinary everyday life, but an alienation from God or one's spiritual source. The fundamental question that preoccupies the sufferer is why? Why is this happening to me? What have I done to deserve this?

This was indeed Job's preoccupation in the *Book of Job* who, through no fault of his own, is subjected to every kind of injustice imaginable with the loss of his possessions and his children and also undergoes grave sickness himself. And, indeed, there seems to be no reason for his degree of suffering. Job challenges God on this and lists the good works he has done in his life. No answer is given on this and the whole concept of Job's suffering remains a mystery.

Pope John Paul emphasizes this mystery of suffering in cases where suffering is not redemptive or punishment for some transgressed divine law. In a sense we limit our understanding of suffering if we hold the mindset that it can only be associated with wrongdoing and punishment. Within this crucible of mystery grows a compassion which is Christ like.

Hinduism perceives suffering as punishment for misdeeds carried out in this lifetime or past ones. As this system of reincarnation accepts karma, a force that determines the quality of each life, Hindus strive to treat others as they themselves would want to be treated. Since humans, according to their individual karma may return in the next life as an animal or insect, Hindus endeavor to foster a respect for all forms of life. They strive to place individual suffering in a broader context of a grand cosmic cycle of birth, life, death and resurrection.

Islamic text translates the very word Islam as 'submission'. To endure suffering and loss is to endure the Will of Allah. Muslims believe that adversity strengthens ones faith. The Qur'an, the actual word of God, mentions numerous incidents of Allah using natural disasters as a way to correct the balance of natural laws or inflict punishment on population; even the prophet Muhammad appealed to Allah for protection against natural disasters.

Judaism holds that suffering is caused by a weakness in one's devotion to God. But rather than being metered out by a punishing God, God suffers alongside the sufferer. The reasons for suffering cannot be comprehended by the finite mind. God's laws are unknowable.

Suffering as Service

Although this only provides a rudimentary template for the meaning of suffering, it is possible to see that where these beliefs are open for individual interpretation, there is a shadow side that can be both dangerous and dark when acted upon by those who take on the Will of God at a personal level without the spiritual maturity to act as a guide. The vision for the freedom of the oppressed may be intuited correctly, but implemented on the wrong level – that of the personality. Ideals can only be correctly implemented if the leaders possess a measure of wisdom to follow it through. We can see this throughout the Christian history of torture and mass genocide in the name of God and martyrdom.

On an individual level, we can harbor powerful and destructive beliefs that are punishing towards ourselves or others and often are untrue. The truth is, with our finite minds, we cannot know the reasons why events have taken place collectively or individually. We can only surmise.

I feel the writing of White Eagle's teaching, through the mediumship of Grace Cooke, holds a very simple and cogent perspective on suffering:

And so, we say to those who suffer – remember, it is not always a question of the working out of karma only. But in the deeper sense it is a way of service, for through suffering and the example of a noble life; others may learn and be helped.

Looking at suffering within the context of service, it is possible to see this historical working out in individual lives where people, through great suffering and loss, birthed works of great worth. Suffering has the rich potential to transform and enrich lives as it can debilitate and imprison the body and mind. And here I would like to use the work of creative artists as a metaphor for giving birth to something from within the darkness as their individual suffering through mental and emotional illness and poverty is apparent in their biographies. But also we can look at the work of Madam Curie and the deprivation she underwent in service of the insight she brought into the world, Helen Keller and her blindness, the life of Beethoven who was to suffer the worst deprivation for a musician – a debilitating and progressive deafness. Then there is Rachel Carson, who wrote that seminal work *Silent Spring* and despite suffering terminal cancer, still spoke her message for the environment which was ridiculed by so many at the time. What emerged from all these voices was the sense of purpose that suffering and hardship forged in these individual lives.

In our modern day we can look at the living artists like Colin Caffell, whose wonderful sculptures were forged out of the dramatic and horrifying loss of his family and Irina Ratushinskaya's remarkable poetry written while imprisoned in Russia.

Service is so often the fruit of suffering in that the sufferer brings insight into the lives of those close to them and opportunities for individual growth. As White Eagle says:

Sometimes physical suffering is accepted by the soul as an opportunity to help others to learn, and to serve. One thinks, for instance, of the parents of a child born with severe handicap, and indeed often the love that the child brings, and the blessing that the parents experience as the result of their own selflessness, as a very rich and priceless gift, and the means of soul growth and expiation of karma.

However, there is a need here to not become a martyr to suffering and abandon any help available for relief of mental and physical pain. Suffering is part of the package of everyday life, but we are not called to suffer for suffering's own sake.

Whether we suffer from depression ourselves or have contact with the depressed through our work as therapists, counselors, relatives or friends, we need to know how to enter into relationship with depression in the right way. For too long, the 'right' way has been perceived from a 'fix-it/cure it/transcend and conquer it perspective'. Although there is nothing potentially wrong with this outlook, it is limiting because of the reductionist theory upon which it rests, where depression is objectified and becomes an 'it' – something to be extracted or acted upon.

But despite this, it is intrinsically difficult to equate depression with soul and even harder to see that depression is an integral part of the spiritual journey. And this is why I want to lead you into the mythical territory of *Persephone and the Underworld*, which has haunted me throughout most of my life. I use myth here to illustrate the journey of depression because myths are essentially ageless and draw us into an inner world which we may only have access to us in our dreams. Myth is a sacred narrative that draws us deep into the realm of spirit and soul.

Chapter 5

Persephone and the Underworld

Whenever I hear that someone is depressed I am reminded of the Underworld and Persephone's passage into the depths in order to find, wisdom, insight and healing. And that is why I refer to it here as both a timeless myth and a very real initiation into the deeper mysteries of life.

When I was nine I was fortunate to find a book in the family library that was in a large enough print for me to read. It was richly illustrated and had once belonged to my uncle; he had won it as a school prize for good attendance. I worked my way through the stories of *Echo and Narcissus, Jason and the Golden Fleece, Theseus and Ariadne, Pandora's Box* and *Cupid and Psyche,* but the story that captivated me the most was *The Story of Persephone.* This began when Demeter, Persephone's mother, who was the Goddess of the Corn, had to journey away from home, as she often did in order to tend the grain, and leaves her beautiful daughter behind for a period of time. Although she had done this before, on this particular occasion she was so reluctant to leave her daughter she was overcome by a deep sadness as if she had a presentiment of what lay before her child. When Persephone understood that her mother wanted to lock her up in a dark cave in order to protect her, she begged her mother to leave her be, assuring her that no harm would come to her and that the merry nymphs, her gentle companions, would look after her. "Oh let me go free, dear mother," she pleaded. Reluctantly, her mother conceded and made her promise to not wander too far.

It was while playing in the meadows with her friends that she was abducted by Pluto, God of The Underworld and held prisoner in his realm against her will. There he married her and, only after much remonstrating from her distraught and bereft mother, who through her grief made the earth barren, was she released for several months of the year. Because she had been enticed into eating the fruit of the Underworld, the pomegranate, she was imprisoned in its depths for four months of the years. During these lonely months, the earth became desolate and cold as the land froze while the bereaved Demeter awaited her beloved daughter's return.

What captured my fascination as a small child were the 'riches' that were held in the depths of the Underworld; Pluto, as God of the Dead, became enriched by all the jewels which were buried with the deceased. I was also fascinated by this world that lay underneath our everyday one. Additionally, as an only child, I empathized with Pluto's lonely vigil in the Underworld. He wasn't unkind, he was just very lonely. When it had come to inheritance, he had suffered a raw deal. While his brothers, Jupiter and Neptune, were King of the Heavens and King of the Seas, respectively, he had drawn the short straw. He was depressed living in a place where his only visitors were the dead. More than anything he longed for a wife and companion. Who wouldn't? As the myth unfolds the reader learns that he is both handsome and rich which is a very potent and beguiling concoction. I think, later, over my years of writing for the romance market, I probably modeled my strong male heroes on Pluto and my heroines on Persephone. Certainly, this has been the successful template for the Mills and Boon romances of the 70's and 80's where the unfortunate heroine is always rescued by a brooding hero of dark and irresistibly handsome looks. The males in these stories always possessed the plutonian element of power and enchantment. Somewhere within me, I probably knew that the pattern of my life would hold a strong underworld theme and this was my attraction to it as a young child. As James Hillman suggests in *The Soul's Code*, the child has a strong intimation of its life destiny from a very early age although this may become lost as the child matures and then picked up later on in life.

The Story

By opening up the myth, I endeavor to unravel the dynamics of the underworld experience. I also look at the nature of will and choice and its hidden presence within depressive illness. Can a profoundly depressed person engage with enough will to make a choice that can move them from a victim stance to one of a hero negotiating a hazardous journey?

Alongside this myth, I want to re-engage with the hero or, in this case, the heroine's journey, specifically focusing on the spiritual nucleus around which the unfolding dynamics constellate. The late mythologist, Joseph Campbell, once a student of Jung, spent a lifetime exploring world myths and traced a distinct pattern emerging through these stories or monomyths. The first 'call to adventure' in his words 'signifies that destiny has summoned the hero and transferred his spiritual centre of gravity from within the pale of his society to a zone unknown.' This region, whether it is in the form of a forest, another world (such as the underworld), an island or mountaintop contains the dual elements of danger and treasure.

We can see this change in 'one's spiritual centre of gravity' underpinning many of our popular contemporary myths. For example, in *Stars Wars*, Luke Skywalker, working on his parent's farm, receives his call to adventure in the form of the beautiful Princess Leia's holographic message appealing to Obi Wan Kenobi for help. As is often the case, the hero initially resists the call and does not cross the threshold which will draw him into direct experience with the otherworld. But then, when he returns to his home, he finds it desecrated and his parents tragically burned to death. In accessing this 'call to adventure', powerful forces that shape the young hero's destiny have been set in motion. The world as he has known it cannot be the same again. His eyes have been opened to another dimension. His strength now lies in the other world and he meets Obi Wan Kenobi who will become his mentor. He has passed through the threshold.

This mythological template underlies the Arthurian legends where the hero is called to go in search of a grail because the land is sick. This is also the prince from 'outside' awakening Sleeping Beauty with a kiss that dislodges the poisoned apple in her throat. It is Jason's call to adventure to seek the Golden Fleece and the quest which confronted Theseus in slaying the Minotaur.

This duplicates, on a psychological level, when the outside world invites the youth to pass through the threshold where his parental guardians keep him unconscious in service of his ultimately safety. Again, there may be levels of resistance before the threshold can be negotiated. These are particularly prominent in our modern day world where there are no rites of passage available or mentors to guide the young soul from the unconscious to conscious participation. Rites of Passage were techniques that allowed the initiate to make the connection with a spiritual guiding force. This was sometimes in the form of an animal totem or mentor that guides him through the threshold. Drugs were used as a way of engaging with a higher state of consciousness and enabling connection with the spiritual axis guiding the youth's first steps in the world. The preoccupation with drugs as panacea for uncomfortable insights struggling to emerge has, sadly, replaced these ancient rites. The danger in this is that the psyche is exposed to too much too soon and becomes like Prometheus who, against spiritual injunctions, steals fire from heaven to give to mortal man. His nemesis was being perpetually tortured by what he had set in motion in the metaphor of being chained to a rock where a raven gorged on his liver by day which was regenerated every night. Prometheus cannot move beyond the bounds of this cyclical tragedy as he has no wise person to help him. Similarly, unsupervised drugs can lock the user into an ongoing addiction so that he is lost in a psychological and spiritual limbo between his old life and the world that awaits him – a world that he lacks the strength and capacity to enter. The only person who can guide him through that threshold is someone who has fallen through the same net and crawled up out of it into the light of day. In this way he can be an invaluable guide to others.

The monomyth has a lot to do with depression, as we will see in the story of Persephone who, seemingly content in her idyllic world, is unconscious to her real destiny, her spiritual axis. Yet, another part of her reaches towards the beguiling narcissus set there to entrap her.

But first I want to take a little look at the nature of will and choice in depressive illness.

Will and Choice

In depressive illness where there is often a loss of personal autonomy and direction with little or no drive to implement even the most rudimentary of tasks, it would seem that the will is not present.

Yet, psychiatrist, Assagioli, cogently defines the will as being a 'function most intimate with the Self'. And if we see that the symptom expressed through the depression is a call of the Self, I firmly believe that the will experienced through the 'I' is present. I initially want to bring my own experience to bear upon this when, one year, when I was deeply depressed and unable to function physically or mentally in the world, I had a clearly defined sense of 'I'. By this I knew that I was ill and that I needed support and I made a choice to admit myself as a voluntary patient into hospital. Despite my inability to even walk without aid, I was aware of what was going on and the dialogue I had with my psychiatrist when we talked about my condition and what my body and mind needed in the way of treatment. Within this intervention, I made an informed choice in service of my Self. During my weeks in hospital I was aware of other patients who, despite their diminished state, were in control of their 'I' and had made similar volitional choices to mine – to put themselves in a place of safety until they were well. In comparison, patients who had been sectioned appeared to have less autonomy and saw their condition as something that was acting on them from outside through the medium of the environment or a destructive relationship.

Time and time again, I have made choices within my recurring illness to seek out help in the form of therapy and medication which will support me through my condition. I conclude that although depression may occlude many facets of the will, such as strength and purpose, where there is a developed sense of 'I' and one can attain some degree of dis-identification from the disturbance, choice enters into the relationship. This choice can be a response to the Self.

This implementation of choice in the midst of debilitating circumstances has been demonstrated throughout history by Dante, for example, in his imprisonment, the Dalai Lama in his exile and Viktor Frankl, the psychiatrist who spent several years in a concentration camp during the war. Frankl believed that the appalling camp conditions were not the sole reason for why a prisoner gave up his will to live. He conceded that whatever debilitating condition people found themselves in they could make a choice of how to respond to this both on a spiritual and mental level. Human dignity, he asserted, was not dependent on outer conditions, but by aligning to a higher purpose. He wrote 'Man can preserve a vestige of spiritual freedom, of independence of mind, even in such terrible conditions of psychic and physical stress.'

Our understanding of the will in the West has been greatly diminished by our preoccupation with its more manifest aspect of doing, acting and asserting. In psychosynthesis, the 'real function of the will is to direct, not impose'. This is very different from our concept of will as a powerful force which, at any cost, needs to be harnessed to drive the personality to achieve its ideals.

Unpacking the Myth

Upperworld
In referring to myth, we are entering what writer and psychologist, James Hillman, refers to as 'depth psychology' which is the interface where mythology and psychology come together.

The story begins with Persephone playing with her friends and gathering flowers that were growing in the nearby meadow. She is away from her mother, Demeter, and the atmosphere is light hearted and jovial. But Persephone is suddenly drawn to a narcissus which enchants her with its beauty and fragrance and she has to have it at all costs. The story describes how this narcissus inspired awe in all who beheld it, but underlying the enchantment lies something more sinister. The narcissus was placed there by Pluto to entrap Persephone.

I would like to suggest that all experiences in life, whether manifesting solely on the outer or inner level, manifest in response to a calling from the Self for greater meaning and purpose. In this context I want to use this as a metaphor that Persephone was reaching for 'something more', something beyond the domain of her experience. Here the narcissus can represent transformation, but as its bloom is beautiful, its roots extend downwards. The key, the reaching for something more, is the impetus that the hero needs to set in motion the forces that will guide him to his destiny. This is the stirring of the 'call to adventure' which will lure the young undifferentiated soul away from parental injunctions that have modeled his reality to one that invites him to be become who he truly is.

This is the threshold we all face when we hear the call of our destiny. It is beguiling and intoxicating as it is dangerous and even terrifying. Yet, to go forward on our journey, our life's quest, we have to navigate this part alone. Our teacher and spiritual mentor can take us to the door as the mother can only take the potential pupil to the school gate or classroom door. But despite the very real threshold fears, once the fragrance and vision of one's destiny has been experienced, ever increasing longing burns within the soul so that the potential hero cannot return to the way he was.

Descent

In reaching for the narcissus Persephone unleashes forces that are too powerful to be resisted. The ground opens and Pluto rides out with his horse and seizes her and carries her with him into the underworld.

Persephone's descent is sudden and brutal as she is dragged against her conscious will into the bowels of the earth. Her passage from the known and familiar into the unknown is a terrifying experience. This violent passage is a known initiatory experience in rites of passage, where young boys approaching manhood are taken away from known and familiar surroundings. There they are subjected to grueling experiences which affect their body, mind and soul. As mythologist Joseph Campbell related in his work; the purpose of this is to jolt them out of their egoic consciousness. They later return as men, changed and wiser. These arduous experiences are essentially genderless and timeless, affecting men and women of all ages and backgrounds. *Separation, descent* and the *unknown* are all components of the hero's journey. Persephone has passed through, or in this case, fallen through the threshold into the otherworld, just as Alice in Wonderland fell down and down into the depths of the rabbit hole.

What actually is the underworld though?

Hillman defines the underworld as that belonging to the soul. The soul is the unconscious and the underworld is all that we exile ourselves from. He urges that 'to know the psyche at its basic depths, one must go to the underworld.' Underworld experiences, whatever form they take, are about loss of the external material world and this is where 'soul-making' takes place. 'The ground of the soul is dark,' writes mystic, Meister Eckhart, and the 'Godhead is dark.'

Descent presents itself in many guises and not necessarily in the form of the sudden and brutal abduction that Persephone suffered. Although descent may seem to suddenly impose itself upon us in the form of an unexpected illness and bereavement, this change agent has been waiting in the wings for some time. We just protect ourselves by going unconscious to it and so descent, when it comes, does seem brutal and unprecedented.

Although the descent into the underworld is experienced very often as being in a state of powerlessness, in that something unknown from the outside has entered our daily life and captured a part of us, the descent very often comes in answer to a call from the Self for greater meaning and depth. Loss and betrayal may be experienced in exploring this myth further. We learn that Persephone's father, Zeus handed her over to his brother, Hades, without her knowledge. On a conscious level, we experience betrayal as our dreams and innocence escape from us, but always this betrayal is in service of something else. On the level of soul there is much to be harvested. Hades' other name, 'Pluto', means riches. Also, as words can be seen as messengers, angels even, in that they convey meaning; in the middle of the word Pluto is 'Lu', who was a God of light and whose presence remains in our vocabulary in describing relationship with light, in words such as lucid and luciferous. Even Lucifer was once a God of light. So in the midst of this Lord of Darkness burns the light that redeems the experience.

In the context of this work, which is about depressive illness, the loss of libido and connection with the solar world of day, which can be a metaphor for the loss of spiritual connection, there is the potential for re-connection on an even deeper level. As Pluto's name conveys, within the darkness is the light. It was in Persephone's reaching for the beautiful flower, for something else, that the door to another world opened.

As Assagioli asserts 'Within the recognition that the descent or fall is a natural happening, affords emotional and mental relief, and encourages the individual to undertake the arduous task of confronting the path to Self realization.' It is in the belief that the experience is just happening to a person in isolation from the rest of humanity, that the pain is felt more keenly. The awareness that this can and does happen on an individual level as well as occurring on a wider collective level calls one to greater meaning. This realisation also serves to strengthen the I-Self connection.

St John of the Cross writes about this type of depression, where there is separation from the spiritual homeland, when he says 'The self is in the dark because it is blinded by a light greater than it can bear...'

Because the majority of suicides are made just before the light begins to enter the experience, in that the darkest hour is before the dawn, it is essential that a spiritual connection is maintained throughout, if possible, either in the form of a trusted person or friend holding this for us or in the simple belief that 'this too shall pass'.

On a less grueling level, the descent can correspond to the frustration stage in the creative process. A work or idea may be aborted here because there appears to be no way forward, no way out. This descent, because of its transformative process, tends to be long in duration from a few weeks to more usually several months or even a year. Soul processes cannot be hurried and are essentially timeless. This is why even a period of a few weeks can appear to be interminable.

Initiation

Although the material about Persephone's experience in the underworld is sparse, the myth does tell us that a marriage took place between her and Pluto. This is synthesis; a marriage between the Lord of the Night and the maiden of the day world; a joining of conscious and unconscious mind. Persephone, in fact, is no longer a girl; she is now a woman and Queen of the Underworld. Something has been lost, but something also has been gained on an intrapsychic level.

Meanwhile, while Persephone is in the underworld, her distraught mother, Demeter, confronts Zeus and adamantly states that if her daughter is not returned, the earth will be barren and mortal kind will perish. The power of the mother of life is strong and uncompromising especially in the face of injustice. Persephone's descent to the underworld is only part of her journey; she still has a life in the upperworld, but because she has eaten the seeds of the pomegranate, a portion of her life is tithed to the underworld. The seeds of wisdom, although partaken of on an unconscious level, multiply and demand our attention as they become conscious. Any challenging period of our life where there is loss on any level, changes us, deepens us, so that we cannot go back to the way we were. Wisdom, depth and soul demand our allegiance in the form of cyclical descents throughout our life. We cannot remain unchanged by an initiation into the underworld. Persephone now has alternatives; a compromise has been reached: she has a work to fulfill in the solar upperworld although she is still married to the Lord of the Underworld.

'From the union of two a third is born,' sounds the old adage. The marriage of Pluto and Persephone has conceived a child. Clarissa Pinkola Estes defines this as anything from 'seeing through new eyes' to a complete change of life direction in the secular world. In the context of this chapter, descents confer a depth of insight into the psyche which will deepen meaning in life. There may be an attunement to a higher sense of purpose, a creative work may be born or maybe the initiate will take up the tools they have gained during their descent and put them to good use in the world.

Descents are, by their nature, essentially creative. Being immersed in the ground of the soul bestows creative wealth on the individual. Pluto is referred to as a 'Lord of Wealth' for good reason. Although there may be loss of innocence and youthful exuberance, the treasures of the soul are there to be utilized and shared. Connection with a spiritual source may have been severed, but largely this severance is in the form of broken dreams, crumbling beliefs which might have served at one time, but have become outdated and a hindrance to further growth.

Return

As the importance of the hero's return is essential in the cycle of completion, so it is with depression. In Gestalt therapy, the work is in making the cycle complete and being able to follow it through on a conscious level. In the face of the underworld experience, in the form of debilitating depressive illness, the hero may, without a strong enough sense of 'I' or unifying centre in the form of a guide or belief, split off from the experience and even go unconscious to it. In this way the fruits of this potentially rich experience never come to light and become locked away so that the hero and, in this case, the depressed person becomes stuck. As the raw unrefined energies split off from consciousness, the initiate can experience a psychotic break where the experience may fragment into memories that return to haunt the person or become locked away somewhere in the unconscious which the personality defends itself heavily against. Opportunities to return and complete this journey appear throughout the life in the form of visions, dreams and quests. The compulsion to complete a journey is a nascent force present in all life, as ultimately there is a drive in every living organism to perfect itself. This underpins the drive in matter to keep repeating experiences until they have completed themselves, reached the end of their journey on their level. Underlying all powerful psychic experiences, where hauntings from the past may become manifest, is the need to complete the journey and live out its potential to completion. This was one Freud, the founder of psychoanalysis, maxims. On a positive note, the journey which for some reason or other could not be completed earlier on in a life or time, because the personality lacked the capacity or strength to contain the experience, will return at a later date. Underworld journeys can occur several times throughout a lifetime.

And so Persephone returns to her mother and the upper-world, but as the myth unfolds, Hades (Pluto) has 'captured' her again by giving her seeds of the underworld fruit, the pomegranate, to eat.

Here, Joseph Campbell, the American mythologist, cogently describes:

The inward journeys of the mythological hero, the shaman, the mystic and the schizophrenic are in principle the same, and when the return or remission occurs, it is experienced as a rebirth, the birth, that is to say, of a twice-born ego, no longer bound by its daylight-world horizon.

Because re-emergence feels so essentially new, almost dazzling, the greatest danger at this point is one of inflation and of attributing the 'awakening' and wisdom gained as belonging to the personality. Contained within the depths are the heights and vice-versa; what goes up comes down. The moment transcendence is engaged with on a purely personal level it becomes demoted to grandiosity which easily punctures. That is why warriors in tribal societies underwent such rigid trials which were essentially there to humiliate. Only through being aware of the unrefined dross of one's lower nature and owning it, can real humility grow. This humility is essential as the tribe will want to project transcendent qualities on the hero which are hard to shrug off.

Perhaps the hero's return can be likened to the honey bee to the hive. The message that he 'dances' within the hive doesn't say 'look how special I am! I come laden with nectar, I am the one'. The honey bee returns from the source already imparting the knowledge to the other bees. It is saying 'What I have found, you too can find if you follow my directions'. It is imperative the receptive bees can work on this knowledge for the survival of the hive. One bee cannot possibly impart all the pollen the colony needs in order to survive. This is also the story of the Christ urging his disciples to walk on the water as a metaphor for the faith they needed to carry out his work: 'Come follow me... I will make you fishers of men...'

In the creative life this stage can be likened to the 'aha' experience where insight reveals itself after an extensive period of incubation. (See Chapter 14).

Digesting the Pomegranate Seeds

Persephone's eating of the pomegranate seeds is a metaphor for the experience she has digested in the underworld. If these seeds had not been partaken of, she would return to the upperworld without any consciousness around the journey she had made and its deeper meaning. Quickly, the memory would fade, be relegated to the unconscious, as if it never happened. As Psychiatrist Bolen asserts 'Eating the seeds meant that Persephone could 'take in' or integrate the experience. It meant that she could now go between the upperworld and the underworld – never again as a victim, but as a guide for others.'

Unless experiences are integrated fully on the levels they impact on, they can seem meaningless. Within depth experiences, transformation is possible; the heart opens and the ethical conscience is awakened so that there is a call to service where the

'I' is in dialogue with the Self.

A Moral Compass

We are in receipt of a 'broken moral compass', concedes spiritual teacher and writer, Ken Wilber. Our old superego injunctions, held in the dominant religion of the time, are no longer holding us in the way they used to. Wilber urges that in our pluralistic culture where everything seems to go and where spiritual values are loosely held, a new morality needs to emerge. This new morality needs to come from within where awakening to the Self becomes the compass to guide us. With nothing outside our desires to bind us, we are desperately in deficit of a spiritual anchoring.

Ecologically, our relentless exploitation of the earth's resources reflects a growing sense of spiritual impoverishment. While one half of the world looks towards acquiring second and third homes, the rest of humanity are eclipsed by growing homelessness which again reflects a sense of spiritual homelessness.

I believe that the only way forward is not through 'flight', which is a term I use for mentally and emotionally splitting off from all the uncomfortable material we find difficult to integrate, but through *descent*, through *deepening*. This cannot be carried out in isolation and is not recommended where the ego may be too fragile to hold the powerful energies released. Rather, this needs to be facilitated by those who know the journey and have some understanding of the cartography within the descent. Few understand this more than those who have traveled and already made that journey. Yet, it is one thing to undergo the experience but another to integrate the material in the psyche. In the case of depression, the most tempting thing to do is split off from the depression, put it behind us in shame and, therefore, refuse the gift it has offered us. This gift makes sense of our depression not as something to be ashamed of but something to be borne with dignity where our wound becomes our teacher. However, the temptation is to feel shame and the very reason why few who have made the 'descent', emerge to become guides through the darkness…

The Light in the Darkness

Very often our most proficient healers are those in need of healing themselves. My work has brought me up against many in the caring profession who invariably struggle with ailments equal to the sick they are attending. Although illness can never be measured ('In a very real sense, we do not cure diseases, they cure us, by restoring our religious participation in life,' writes Jungian psychologist, Thomas Moore), the wound itself becomes the lens through which we engage with and can see the 'other'. Old wounds become scars and we are apt to go to sleep unless we have that edge to keep us awake in the form of the wound that does not heal.

As the Dalai Lama suggests, 'It is not enough to be compassionate, you must act…' Acting in the right way, in dialogue with the Self, has direct benefit on the situation whether it be on a local or global level.

'To integrate an experience of suffering is an act of consciousness,' writes psychiatrist, Bolen. I would also add that it is an act of conscience, an awakening of moral imperative to enable others to negotiate the dark realms within themselves – to be a guide.

No journey can be made without provisions to see us through challenging and lean times. The next chapter section, *Tools on the Journey*, explores the role of medication and counseling in alleviating the anguish of deep and unremitting depression. Hopefully, by debunking some of the myths and mindsets about medication, the reader can make an informed choice regarding medication and counseling.

PART II

Chapter 6

Tools on the Journey

Medical Intervention

Desperation is usually the factor that sends the depressed person to the GP for help. The decision to invite medical intervention is not taken on lightly. Additionally, powerful societal mindsets about taking medication to relieve negative states of mind can further prolong the process. This is especially so in men, where there will be more powerful injunctions in place of not becoming dependent on a prop, the danger of losing control and becoming biologically manipulated. For a number of years, before the physiological addiction to barbiturates and tranquillizers became common knowledge, it wasn't unusual for men to self-medicate their depression with barbiturates in the form of sleeping tablets and alcohol, while women self- medicated with the popular 1950s benzodiazepines like Valium and Librium. For men, taking something for lack of sleep due to an overactive mind or work stress was much more acceptable than resorting to antidepressants which were seen as a form of weakness and failure.

Here, I want to re-introduce the importance of maintaining the awareness of depression being a spiritual journey and including medication as part of that journey. All I would ask you to do at this point is be aware of any mindsets, thoughts or visceral feelings you may bring to this chapter, make a note of them and be aware of how they can capture any impartiality you may need as you read. Often, if we do not acknowledge these powerful thoughts and feelings at their onset, they can take over and occlude any true and clear understanding of what is being presented. Be aware that, this chapter more than any other, can evoke powerful feelings and insights that are based on societal injunctions that have been in existence for several hundred years. Anything that remotely challenges these mindsets will evoke a strong reaction in the psyche.

My Own Experience

My first introduction to the medical model came when I was nineteen. I was six months into my student training in working with people with learning difficulties and I had been deeply depressed the last three of them. Nothing in particular had precipitated my descent as I had, up until then, enjoyed my work at the hospital. Set on the North Welsh coast, it had the advantage of both sea in the foreground and mountains in the background. I loved the landscape and I had a good relationship with my fellow students and the tutors who taught the course. More than anything, I enjoyed working on the various units and getting to know the residents, taking them out on walks and supporting them in their development of life skills. It could be challenging work, but it was also rewarding as patients came to trust me as a friend as well as a helper.

For several months I had struggled on my own, battling the usual symptoms of sleeplessness, loss of appetite, lethargy and low self esteem that shadows such an illness. Eventually, a friend and colleague whom I trusted very much suggested I sought medical intervention as it had helped her during university when she had exams.

Although she had warned me of the side effects and the initial period where physiological symptoms of being slowed down and feeling drugged would be at the worst, I couldn't tolerate them for more than ten days and then I flushed them down the toilet. I was working on speech therapy at the time and my speech was slurred and I felt awful. Somehow I got through the depression, helped along by a boyfriend, a young psychologist who was incredibly patient with me and wouldn't allow me to sink too deeply into depression. Instead of denying my suicidal feelings by steering me onto another subject, he accepted them and somehow I held on until one day I woke up after a normal night's sleep and found that I was well again.

The Healing Field

I wasn't to try medication again until in my thirties when I was undergoing a major life change of moving to another country, going through a divorce and starting up life there. All this was in the midst of suicidal depression. This time a trusted friend, who was also a healer, held my visit to the doctor in the 'light'. She lit a candle and both of us asked that I may be guided to the right doctor and medication. She referred to this process as 'the healing field'. Defining this, the word 'field' replaced the word soul. As, scientist, Sheldrake proposes, 'Fields are invisible organising fields of nature.' Every life form that enters incarnation is held within a 'soul'.

Although I had been plagued by deep unrelenting anxiety for weeks, I experienced a peace when I entered the doctor's surgery. He listened to me carefully and with an empathy that was almost tangible. He warned me of the initial side effects of the medication and recommended that I needed to stick with them and to come back and see him in two weeks time. I didn't have to ask him, but he offered to write me off work for several months. I visited him until the medication kicked in and I began to feel the depression lift and my energy return. He confided in me that he had suffered bouts of debilitating depression himself throughout his life and that he had found this particular medication useful. More than anything I was aware of his empathic resonance which only really comes from a fellow sufferer, but also the sense of peace that pervaded the surgery when I entered it.

My friend, on asking how my visit went, admitted that she too had experienced a great peace and reminded me that when someone is receiving healing, the patient and their problem comes under a particular healing ray which will, like a magnet, draw the help, people and conditions which will best serve the patient towards them. I do believe this to be so and I was able to surrender my healing process to something greater than myself. Since then, when seeking medical intervention for my condition, I have held the situation within the 'healing field' and I have always found the right medical intervention has arrived. What I want to illustrate here is that there is not a wrong or a right way to treat depressive illness. If it is held within the healing field, then intervention comes in the way that is most helpful to the subject. In being open to medical and psychological intervention, if held within a spiritual context, the help arrives. The only barriers I have found to this are mindsets and prejudice to the type of process divinely invited.

Experiencing depression being held within a larger field of healing has enabled me to work with the problem, or dis-ease, rather than against it – and to ultimately write this book.

From a therapist's standpoint it is so important that a patient's choice of medical intervention for their condition is supported rather than fought. A therapist or healer's prejudice to a particular method of treatment says more about their own mindsets than that of the patient!

Because medication works to compensate for glitches and anomalies in the technology of the brain, we need to understand how and why these occur. I will explain the role of neurons and neurotransmitters and what happens when there is a breakdown in communication between these components. Also, what happens when the right medication is introduced.

Serotonin and Depression

Since the advent of Selective Serotonin Reuptake Inhibitors (SSRIs) in the 1980's, principally Prozac, serotonin has become a buzz word in connection with depression. The SSRIs work on maintaining serotonin in the nerve cells by demobilizing their breakdown. You can even buy serotonin from mail order catalogues that deal in health products, or in the form of L-Tryptophan which is the precursor of serotonin. Serotonin supplements are pretty useless on their own because they fail to cross the blood brain barrier. This is a protective measure that prevents potentially toxic chemicals from entering the brain. Tryptophan can navigate this barrier. However, there are various chemical substances that are small enough to slip through this barrier, such as alcohol, nicotine and ecstasy, and can do real damage.

Foods that are rich in serotonin, such as oats, sunflower and pumpkin seeds can be beneficial unless there is a problem with absorption in the neurons. Similarly antidepressants that target the serotonin receptors are little use if there is no serotonin in the brain to target.

Serotonin is basically a neurotransmitter sometimes known as the 'happiness brain chemical' because a high level of serotonin is equated with wellbeing, social inclusion and extroversion. According to studies and research into animal and human behavior, depression, lethargy and slowed mental and motor function are associated with low levels of serotonin. Evidence has been found of this by taking samples of blood and cerebral spinal fluid from depressed patients. Also, autopsies that have been carried out on suicides reveal the same; that the serotonergic neural system is faulty in some way to even being atrophied.

Why then do some people have healthy serotonergic systems and others have impaired ones?

Some psychiatrists who have carried out a lot of research, like the late American psychiatrist and spiritual counselor, Gerald May, believe that a healthy serotonergic system is largely hereditary and passed on in the genes intergenerationally. Certainly, there is a strong hereditary factor in psychiatric illness as in other types of illnesses like cardiac ones, the cancers and muscle and skeletal degenerative disorders. And here this evokes the nature-nurture dilemma as, alongside these lie historical events in the child's life which deplete serotonin levels, like abandonment, death of a parent or prolonged emotional and physical abuse.

Clinical psychologist, Oliver James, has dedicated a whole book, *Britain on the Couch*, to the exploration of what he refers to as 'a low serotonin society'. He based his finding on a scientific study of vervet monkeys whose serotonin levels were high if they were dominant and low if they became subservient to others. He places this thesis alongside the factual theory that depression has escalated out of all proportion since the 1950's and is increasing. His research into the lives of his patients over the years revealed that the drive to capitalism, to having more, was the impetus behind feelings of failure and depression. Basically, capitalism stokes the fires of discontent because our society is brainwashed into believing that if we upgrade our status, financially and on a career level, we will feel happier and more fulfilled. We can see the rationale behind this in the way the media accentuates the glamour and life of our celebrities. The myth the media and many of us support is 'If we become rich and famous, then our problems will be over.' This overall inability to reach the psychosocial goalposts of our time and the resulting sense of failure and low self esteem feeds into the low serotonin, low status loop. He writes:

Put crudely, advance capitalism makes money out of misery and dissatisfaction, as if it were encouraging us to fill the psychic void with material goodness. It can also profit from fostering spurious individualism by encouraging us to define ourselves through our purchases, with ever more precisely marked products that create a fetishist concern to have 'this' rather than 'that', even though there is often no significant practical difference.

Although Oliver James' insights are valuable and compelling they, like all insights, only form part of the picture. The underlying problem is in displacing our spirituality, our sense of the divine onto objects and idols which we worship and attach ourselves too. We freely subscribe to a culture that mirrors our lack and we believe in it because we choose to, not because we have to because our life depends on it. Instead, our illusionary status depends on it. In subscribing to this belief, we have become unconscious to our true divine status.

If our psychosocial environment is not the only culprit in jettisoning our self esteem, modern science points to the theory that we are adversely affected by electro-magnetic radiation which depletes melatonin levels. Melatonin is produced during nocturnal sleep and is a powerful antioxidant which has a direct effect on serotonin levels. I have a close friend who, after being near power lines, mobile phones or computers for any length of time, cries for a whole day afterwards because she feels so depressed. Our neurochemistry is sustained by electrical impulses from nerve cell to nerve cell, from thought, to memory, to imagination and creativity. Oliver James cites 'Thoughts are electro-chemical events.'

We administer electrical shock treatment (defibrillation) to the heart to kick-start it into going again or stop an abnormal and potentially fatal rhythm. We trace the heart's electrical pathway using an electrocardiogram (ECG) so that we can determine if there is a problem. Similarly, in particularly resistant depressions that fail to respond to drug therapy, electroconvulsive therapy is administered to the brain. Several sessions of this over a period of time somehow kick-starts the brain into working again. Despite public horror around this treatment, it is considered to be highly effective in the long term for depression. My work has brought me into contact with a number of people who have greatly benefited from this and genuinely look upon it as a life saver. The gentle way isn't always the right one as nature demonstrates in its raging tempests, volcanic eruptions and earthquakes that shatter landscapes as well as lives. And yet there are some seeds that can only grow after a fire has ravaged the land. The Black Spruce, which grows throughout Newfoundland and Alaska, can only propagate through fire. The heat opens the cones so that the seeds are spilled and continue to disperse several years post-fire. Fire releases valuable nutrients from the woody matter in the form of nitrogen and ash, which fertilizes the ground ready for germination.

American psychiatrist, Peter Kramer, includes an interesting piece by a researcher about serotonin:

Maybe serotonin is the police. The police aren't in one place – they're not in the police station. They are a presence every- where. They are cruising the city – they are right there. Their potential presence makes you feel secure. It allows you to do many things that also make you feel secure. If you don't have enough police, all sorts of things happen. You may have riots. The absence of police does not cause riots. But if you do have a riot, and you don't have police, there is nothing to stop the riot from spreading.

Neurotransmitters and the Role of Neurons

Basically, neurotransmitters are the brain's messengers. If they fail to function adequately communication breaks down. We can see how this happens in Parkinson's disease where there is a deficit in the neurotransmitter dopamine which directly affects mobility. A deficiency here involves loss of control of small motor movements and the tremor, so reminiscent of the disease. The introduction of L-dopa, which is the precursor of dopamine, alleviates the distressing symptoms of Parkinson's. Additionally, mania in bipolar disorder is said to be caused by excessive dopaminergic activity.

It was actually in the 1950s that noradrenalin and serotonin were discovered along with dopamine. These three chemical substances became known as the 'monoamines' and were directly related to mood. Around about this time, several other drugs which seemed to have an elevating effect on mood were created. These were Iproniazid and Imipramine and were used in the treatment of depression. They worked by controlling the functioning of neurotransmitters. These earlier drugs were designed to target noradrenalin and dopamine.

To appreciate how the neural traffic system works, we need to understand a little about neurons, the nerve cells themselves. Basically, the brain consists of over a 100 billion neurons which make up the grey matter of the outer cortex. Each neuron has an axon which connects all the grey matter together. An axon may vary in length according to locality of the areas it is influencing in the brain tissue. These axons form the white matter of the brain. Obviously, imbalances in the white matter seriously undermine our ability to make connections.

At the end of the axon the neurons forms dendrites which, rather like the roots of a tree, divide and multiply as designated by their particular purpose. To grasp the magnitude of this networking we need to remember that each nerve cell, of which there are billions, have on average *twenty thousand synapses each*! At the end of each dendrite is the synapse or synaptic cleft across which the neurotransmitter sends its message to be picked up by the receptors of another cell. Successful transmission across this synaptic cleft is absolutely vital both from the sender to the receiver.

We know how important lucidity and clarity is in our land and mobile phone communication system; if the line is faulty, the message we are sending and receiving is compromised. Those of us involved in networking through email understand how important it is that everyone on the network receives and responds to the messages being sent or important points get missed; people get missed and this can lead to no end of frustration, ambivalence and resentment due to faulty assumptions. When the communication system works at an optimal level, then we say 'things seem to flow'.

The sensitivity of the brain's network system is a metaphor for the sensitivity of our interpersonal communications in the world. Messages between nerve cells in the brain are electrical events involving a complexity of chemical reactions which take place automatically.

The biological theory is that if the neurotransmitters are broken down too quickly in the synapse, then their work in maintaining homeostasis between nerve cells is undermined. Since a neurotransmitter's function is to stimulate, inhibit or facilitate a cell's activity, obviously there is some deficit in this involuntary process. The effect of the SSRIs is to inhibit the breakdown of the neurotransmitters.

My love of metaphors makes it impossible to resist using the one here of the neural network of the brain as being a rich one for the complexity and connectivity of our biosphere. From the ant, piece of plankton, to the elephant and whale, everything is connected. Each food chain is dependent on another and if one of these vital components, rather like Russian dolls that nest inside each other, becomes extinct, it affects us all. Our work, our life, becomes compromised or enhanced by the quality of the network that supports us on a biological as well as interpersonal level. Like the inner homeostasis of the neural network, nervous system and complete bodily system, homeostasis globally can only be maintained by our cooperation in the process as environmental statistics reveal. Consciousness around this is increasing at a crucial time in our planetary evolution. We have to start making the connections between what we do intrapsychically, interpersonally and ecologically if we are to prevent the atrophying of our planet. We cannot harm that which supports us without harming ourselves.

Depression and the Brain

It is not just the neural traffic that is compromised by a chemical imbalance. There are areas of the brain that are particularly sensitive to our mood and emotion. This is to such a great extent that we have to ask ourselves the questions of what comes first; the behavior (nurture) or the genes (nature)? Rather than polarize towards one theory in favor of the other and continue sustaining an ageless dichotomy, I want to include both.

There is ample scientific evidence to suggest that in severe depression there is less activity in the brain. Cortical functioning is reduced and using a process of brain imaging and research carried out during post mortem studies of brain tissue, insights have emerged that depression not only weakens neural networks but also causes brain tissue to atrophy, particularly in the prefrontal cortex. This area has a direct effect on personality and has been referred to as the neurological seat of the conscience. So, as Rita Carter, author of *Mapping the Mind*, writes 'The depressed person is without drive or desire to do anything, yet is abnormally fixated on their intense emotional state'. Similarly, the feelings of emotional deadness, so symptomatic of deep depression, are often due to inactivity in the parietal and upper temporal lobes that are related to attention and what is going on in the world in current affairs.

In short, the world of the depressed person shrinks and everything outside brings a sense of unreality and alienation that is frightening. Because the amygdala, the bodily alarm system, is affected, the depressed person can feel as if they are swamped by feelings of deep unremitting anxiety, fear and guilt. The amygdala shares robust neural connections to the older limbic brain. Here activity is largely unconscious and can be overwhelming. It is interesting that working on cognitive mental tasks inhibits the somewhat emotional content of the amygdala and this is why cognitive therapy can be so helpful in alleviating some of the symptoms of depression and focusing the mind on future goals (see Chapter 7).

The other area affected by depression is the hypothalamus. The part that deals with recent memories, especially emotionally charged memories, is smaller in people with depression. Psychiatrist, Kramer, writes about this and describes cases where high resolution magnetic imaging has revealed this. At first, this hippocampal shrinkage was thought to be something which happened with age. This would explain the heightened statistics of depression amongst the elderly. But hippocampal damage was found to be evident in depressed people that were both young and old. In short, depression caused the hippocampal shrinkage.

Glial Cells – the Glue

Neurons are embedded in a supportive matrix of glial cells which make up the external structure of the brain. 'Glial' derives from the Greek word for glue. They literally are the glue which maintains a healthy environment for the neurons. Basically, the glia makes up approximately 90 percent of the cells in the brain and account for half the brain's weight. Until recently, the glia were assigned a relatively passive role in contrast to the active neurons they support. But researchers at Stanford University believed that they are largely responsible for the correct wiring in the brain. With sufficient glia around, connectivity between the neural networks rarely failed. They are crucial in the formation of strong synapses as the brain develops. Physiologists at the University of Minnesota discovered that when glial cells are prodded, they release calcium ions which, in turn, stimulate the glia to release glutamate, a neurotransmitter used by neurons to communicate with one another.

In the context of neurodegenerative conditions like depression, Alzheimer's and Huntingdon's disease, there is a deficiency in glial cells. Similarly, studies have shown that people suffering from depression have a deficit of these glial cells which can seriously undermine synaptic growth and neuronal activity. Kramer, who carried out a lot of research in this area, believed that these glial cells were protective and acted as a buffer to various stressors. When these glial cells were deficient there was not sufficient cushioning to act as a shield against an onslaught of stressful situations. Glial cells increase resilience to vulnerability.

One of the main types of glia are the star-shaped astrocytes which clean up toxins and debris in the brain and transport nutrients to neurons. Further research in neuroscience has revealed that the presence of astrocytes can alleviate the damage cause by stroke as their role of closing the gaps lessens secondary brain death. Additionally, they have the capacity to instruct stems cells to become neurons.

Antidepressants

There are three main types of antidepressants available today: the Triyclics, MAOIs and the newer 'cleaner' ones, the SSRIs. They are all 70 percent effective if taken properly, have various side effects that may be helpful to some people, and less helpful to others and all are targeted to act on several neurotransmitters that have a direct effect on mood and bodily functions.

Most people are concerned about how addictive drugs are, becoming stuck on them for ever, or about their side effects. And here I want to include my own experience of medication alongside valuable research and direct contact with other people.

Antidepressants, in themselves, are not addictive in the same way as the benzodiazepines, such as Valium and Librium. But, because they can make you feel well, you may feel that you don't need them any more. And this may be so, but often a too sudden tailoring off of medication can bring about a relapse. Giving up medication should be done slowly and incrementally. I have met an alarming amount of patients who have stopped their medication too quickly and ended up in hospital as a result of a suicide attempt or other acts of self harm. A sudden relapse can be more disturbing than the actual symptoms before. It should be remembered that depression is a serious debilitating condition as potentially life threatening as diabetes, cardiac problems, and cancer. Sometimes, just feeling well can be a sign that the medication is working. The guilt about taking medication may need to be addressed rather than the efficacy of a drug. The decision to take medication can bring up all sorts of issues around pride, autonomy, control and ambivalence towards being dependent on a chemical substance.

Tolerance can be mistaken for addiction in that, with time, the body becomes acclimatized to a particular medication so more is needed. Increasing the dose may be affective and legitimate for a while until a decision is made between you and the GP whether you want to continue increasing the dose or try something else. Since everyone is different, there is no guarantee that a drug will cease to be affective with time. Some people can take a medication for a number of years without having to increase their medication or change it. One of the main precursors to medication failing or not being as affective is an increasing stress level in the person's life. Even when you are well and perhaps especially so because your defenses are down, you are vulnerable to stress.

It is not possible to discuss medication without including your GP because their experience, insight, understanding or lack of it will influence your choice. Like anything, there are doctors that are sympathetic and have more than a perfunctory interest in depression, and there are others who are unsympathetic and antagonistic towards mental illness. To be fair, doctors are not psychiatrists, but they are expected to be because of the one in four depressed people who enter their surgery. A doctor who is honest about his shortcomings in this area can be infinitely more helpful by referring his depressed patients to a psychiatrist rather than imposing mindsets on those who have come to him for help. The problem is that depression can be either precipitated by psychological problems or biological ones or a combination of both. I have to say that for someone who has moved around a lot, abroad and in this country, I have encountered many good doctors who have an understanding of the magnitude of depressive illness. These, I have found, have either admitted to depressive illness themselves or have had relations, colleagues or close friends who suffer from it. The doctor I have now firmly believes that many people suffer from a serotonin deficiency. Although he does not suffer from depression himself, he is aware of its gravity through fellow colleagues. By the same token, there are sympathetic psychiatrists and less sympathetic psychiatrists.

The inclusion of the healing field here is of paramount importance when visiting a representative of the medical profession. And we may need to remind ourselves that the person sitting behind the desk is more than a label; he or she is a human being and a soul whom we have invited to travel with us on our journey. I have always found that including the situation in the healing field creates the right ambience for the meeting with 'experts' who can otherwise seem daunting. Often it is not what is or isn't said in the consulting room but the unspoken silence. Remember, if we go in to see the doctor or expert with mindsets based on preconceived ideas or history, the 'other' will respond to these mindsets in their own way. The diagnosis of a condition, although informed by knowledge and skill, is largely dependent on intuition coming to the fore as well. Mindsets and resentments can seriously impede the flow of intuition. Like anything, going for a consultation to a representative of their field – whether it is medical, psychiatric or business – is part of a process. We can enable the process to come into being by being conscious of the 'space' we are creating. Just because we may have had a negative experience in the past with a doctor or psychiatrist, it doesn't mean this is going to be the same within the next encounter.

I want to briefly cover the three types of medication used for depression along with their benefits and common side effects.

SSRIs (Selective Serotonin Reuptake Inhibitors)
Prozac has been the star and forerunner of the SSRIs which came onto the market in the 1980s. Basically, they inhibit the neuro-transmitter, serotonin, from being taken up by the body too quickly, by keeping the serotonin in the synaptic cleft for a longer period. That way, the receptors at the end of the neurons have more opportunity to absorb and pass on the chemical. In depressed people there is usually a faulty serotonergic system that prevents serotonin from being passed between the nerve cells efficiently.

Although serotonin has been targeted by the earlier tricyclic antidepressants, the SSRIs because of their fine tuning have less likelihood of toxic side effects. For this reason, they are often the preferred medication when prescribing for potentially suicidal patients. Additionally, besides alleviating depression, they are found helpful for young people with various psychological conditions like self-harming, anorexia nervosa, obsessive compulsive disorder (OCD), anxiety and personality disorders.

SSRIs include Prozac (fluoextine), Seroxat (paroxetine), Lustral (sertraline) and Cipramil (citalpram). Prozac's popularity has been largely because its side effects are few and it seems to be an all-rounder. It is extremely effective in mobilizing energy and releasing one's get up and go. I have taken Prozac for two years now and apart from an initial adaptation period of a few weeks I have found it by far the best medication for me. It pulled me from the brink of suicide and despair. I felt more myself than I had in some years. I can honestly say that without Prozac's efficacy I would not be alive today. Although I have to add, because of my level of despair, it took six weeks to become fully affective!

There are far fewer side effects with SSRIs than with other types of antidepressants, once the initial adaptation period has been negotiated. The initial and more common sensations are nausea, loss of appetite, dizziness and feeling spaced out. Also, like most antidepressants there may be disturbances to the libido.

There has been a lot of negative publicity about the SSRIs, mainly that they can evoke suicidal feelings especially in the early stages. I feel I want to add here that in deep depression, it is often impossible to find the will to mobilize and act out any disturbing feelings. The critical stage, as all psychiatrists and most doctors know, is at that point where the depressed person is beginning to get better and feelings are flooding back. And this is why a doctor needs to closely monitor their patient's progress.

Incidentally, the hidden benefits of SSRIs, particularly Prozac, is their ability to promote neurogenesis: the growth of new brain cells. This has got to be a good thing as deep and prolonged depression causes brain tissue to atrophy. Like the Tricyclics, they also have a positive effect on alleviating irritable bowel syndrome.

Tricyclics

These have been around a lot longer than the SSRIs and were developed in the 1950s. Their name is derived from their molecular constitution in which the atom was made up of three rings. The tricyclics work by inhibiting the re-uptake of the neurotransmitters – norepinephrine, dopamine or serotonin – by nerve cells.

The first one to emerge by chance was Iproniazid which was a drug used initially in the treatment of tuberculosis. While improving appetite and generally aiding the constitution, it was noticed that people who took it became 'inappropriately happy'. Iproniazid became used as one of the first affective antidepressants marketed in 1958. It was regarded as a psychic energizer.

The calming sedative effects are experienced immediately, and they are highly effective where depression is anxiety based. Despite the recent advent of SSRIs, the tricyclics are still popular with many older people. The main ones are Dothiepin, Clomapramil and Amytriptiline. Dothiepin was my first introduction to an effective antidepressant and I found it very helpful for some months in calming me and helping me to sleep when my stress levels were very high.

Because they can elevate blood pressure, they are not recommended for people with cardiac problems. Also, because they can trigger off a manic episode they are not usually recommended in bipolar disorder. Initial side effects are blurred vision, dry mouth, drowsiness and difficulty urinating. These symptoms may persist as dosage is increased.

The hidden benefits of the tricyclics are in their various pain relieving qualities, especially in neuromuscular pain and in alleviating irritable bowel syndrome.

MAOIs

Monomine oxidase is an enzyme found in the human body which, in the brain, breaks down neurotransmitters such as serotonin and norepinephrine. Monoamine Oxidase Inhibitors (MAOIs) put the brakes on this enzyme action and raise the level of neurotransmitters which elevates the mood; although they are highly effective, because of their toxic interaction with certain foods, they are often not a first choice of antidepressant. They are used sometimes as a last resort for those resistant to the tricyclics and SSRIs. The foods they interact with are ones containing the amino acid, tyramine, which can contribute to high blood pressure. Since tyramine is found in red wine, particularly

Chianti, liver, fava beans, marmite and other yeast based spreads, it poses a sustained vigilance on what one eats which might not always be possible in the face of illness. These older drugs include Phenalzine and Parnate. But with the advent of newer MAOIs there are fewer side effects. More recently a patch can be worn whose absorption doesn't interfere with digestion.

MAOIs are particularly effective for depression where there are symptoms of overeating, sleeplessness and anxiety. One of their hidden benefits is their efficacy in curbing the desire to smoke.

As in all antidepressant medication it is important that they are not mixed, and if they are that this is done on the advice of a GP or psychiatrist who is aware of the various contraindications.

Lithium

This is the lightest of the solid elements and, because of this, is believed to have possessed 'modest magical qualities.'

Although lithium carbonate has been around since the 1940s and like so many successful chemicals was discovered largely by chance, it is used very effectively today in the treatment of bipolar disorder. It is a natural salt of glutamic acid, the main excitatory neurotransmitter for all nerve impulses in the mammalian brain. Its role here has been to stabilize the mood swings from suicidal depression to mania. American Psychiatrist, Kay Redfield Jamieson, praises its efficacy both in her life in treating her bipolar disorder and also in its use as an antisuicide medication. She believes its efficacy is due to its 'capacity to enhance serotonin turnover in the brain' as well as aiding the efficacy of other neurotransmitters. As an end result of this, there is a decrease in aggression, agitation, depression and mania.

I talked to a colleague who suffered from bipolar disorder and had been on lithium for several years and he likened it to a seatbelt he needed to wear when he was traveling through life.

He described it as keeping him just short of flying too high or falling like Icarus back into the sea. He said it just kept his chin above the floor when he plunged into a downward spiral.

Although lithium works very well, it does need to be monitored regularly through routine blood tests as too little of it can be ineffective and too higher dose can be toxic. By the same token, it does not necessarily suit everyone although there are many claims that it can be a miracle drug. A study in the late 1990s in Sweden revealed that statistically there was as much as a 77 percent reduction in suicide when taking lithium. This is quite remarkable.

Side Effects

Although it is important that we don't become overwhelmed by the possible side effects of a medication, it is common sense accepting that there will be some initial side effects while the medication is entering into the bodily system. That is why a relatively low and ineffective dose is introduced initially. Side effects can be equated with the new pair of glasses or contact lenses which we need to accommodate, or the supportive arches in our shoes, both of which appear to exacerbate the underlying condition initially rather than make it better.

To look at side effects more realistically we should not isolate this from the side effects or collateral we can suffer when we do anything different. Medication is by no means isolated in this. If we go to the gym after a long period away or take up jogging, we will experience aching and sore muscles until our body acclimatizes to the new form of exercise. Acclimatization is often worse in the first few weeks. If we take up studying after a long period away we will experience tiredness and the sense of being overwhelmed by the sheer volume of information until our bodily system adapts. If we take up full time work again after a break, we are bound to feel stressed and exhausted for the first few weeks until we become familiar with the working environment. Because we have an innate dislike for these unpleasant side effects we may become discouraged after the first few weeks and convince ourselves that the bad effects outweigh the good and give up. In order to continue an activity that appears to be taking more out of us than we are getting back, we need to keep aligned to purpose, meaning and values. Just one of these will enable us to find the will to carry it through. If our purpose, in this context, is to feel less depressed, we have to put up with the initial side effects such as increased anxiety or feeling sedated. Most of the time, it will pass, and this is why our GP will advise we call back in ten days after we have commenced the medication in order to monitor our progress. The first two weeks are the critical phase where we may actually feel worse before we feel better. This is true also of many complementary therapies such as homeopathy, when we may actually feel worse to begin with, or other deep seated problems may re-surface; these are side effects too – initial ones that pass as time goes by.

Basically, all antidepressants take time to have a tangible positive effect. This can be anything from 10 days to 6-8 weeks. If one is in a critical state of depression and cannot tolerate waiting for such a long period because of high levels of anxiety making sleeping and eating impossible, the GP or psychiatrist might prescribe a short period of tranquillizers until the anti-depressants have kicked in. And providing the patient isn't suicidal, this can be a very reliable way to make things run more smoothly. I have experienced this passage into antidepressants myself and found it very effective and did not feel addicted in any way after the tranquillizers had run their course. This saved me a lot of unbearable anxiety.

Why Medication doesn't Always Work

Any psychiatrist will say that one of the reasons why medication doesn't always work is because only 3 out of 5 of people follow the instructions. The advice here is to *give them a chance to work!*

Reasons for this are because people think they can self-medicate; for example, they might begin to feel worse and after a few days discontinue the tablets. Others may feel ashamed of taking medication and cut down indiscriminately to make themselves feel better about taking them. I have known people resort to just taking one antidepressant *now* and *then*! Sadly, antidepressants are not like narcotics or tranquilizers with an immediate effect. Still others will, after feeling better, give up their medication thinking they are cured. Another simple reason why medication may not work is because the dose is not high enough for the person, or in some cases is too high.

Sometimes doctors that have no real empathy or under-standing of the condition will get someone to cut down before they are ready, putting them on a maintenance dose. In this sense, not all doctors know what they are doing. I have found the wiser ones will admit this and enter into a dialogue with the patient and their relatives so that it can be a shared responsibility.

And here I do want to stress the importance of having a mentor or friend with you when visiting your GP. In this way, the depressive whose mental, emotional and psychological factors are greatly reduced has the support of a mentor. This is basically someone who knows and understands the patient and can fill in important details of the condition which may be easily overlooked in the midst of a stressful situation where time is in short supply.

The other reason why medication doesn't always work is because the medication may not suit the person or can interact adversely with other medication. Like anything, getting the right medication is a process of trial and error which requires patience and persistence.

What to do when a Medication does Work
Stay on the medication!

Although this may be obvious, it is amazing how many people

decide its time to jack in the course of treatment! This is like sailing into calmer waters after a rather terrifying storm and then, after no time at all to reassess the situation or draw up preventative measures, heading straight out into the storm again!

And it is worth remember here that rather than medication being a last resort or the end of the road, it may actually mark the beginning of accepting better health and a stability which enables long term plans to be made. Making long term plans may not have been possible before. Certainly, this has been true for me.

The Difficulty in Accepting Medication

The journey from being medication-free to taking medication is one riddled with apprehension, resistance, ambivalence and desperation. The idea that depressed or anxious people mindlessly pop pills without foresight or consideration for the long term consequence is a complete myth. Taking medication is not only a loss of personal autonomy and self esteem, but also an admission that one has a genuine medical condition that warrants treatment. Powerful feelings that may have closed the door to treatment before become axed and there are feelings of shame and failure that one doesn't have what it takes to cope with oneself any more.

The movement from non-medication to medication is a non-linear process. It is based on escalating, progressively more debilitating depressive episodes to ever diminishing spates of relative normality when the dis-ease's intensity is rationalized away or even flatly denied. This can take place over months, but more usually years, even decades. Within this process there may be visits to the GP with an assortment of vague, seemingly unrelated symptoms, such as disturbed sleep pattern, lethargy, exhaustion and anxiety. The patient in denial may be an expert in colluding with those around him, including the doctor to support the conviction that they need a holiday, a rest from work or a change of job. If depression is suggested to be the possible cause of symptoms, it is rigorously dismissed. Powerful defense mechanisms will be in place to discourage or cut dead even the suggestion of depressive illness. Furthermore, even the barest suggestion of depressive illness may send the visiting patient scurrying off to try out an assortment of deflective pursuits; anything from doing a college course, going to the gym, or seeking out the help of alternative health practitioners, all of whom may serve to alleviate the depression temporarily (physical exercise is a known method of treatment for depression and embarking on a college course stimulates cortical functions which are known to soothe anxious thoughts).

Even though antidepressants in the 1980s, in the form of Prozac, the first SSRIs, were less riddled with unpleasant side effects, people were still reluctant to admit they were taking antidepressants, even though they might have crossed that threshold from being medication-free to taking medication.

The insights of sociologist David Karp are important here when describing the protracted and often painful process that leads to taking medication. He refers to this as an 'evolution in illness consciousness' which is manifested through four successive states. These are *Resistance, Trial commitment, Conversion* and *Disenchantment*.

Resistance

Resistance obviously manifests in the form of what I have been writing about where denial, ambivalence and anger towards ones own powerlessness keep one away from medication. Various other reasons would be a concern about the long term effect of taking medication based on information from colleagues, friends and family and the very sobering effect of the media on highlighting the defects and horror stories linked with prescriptive medication. Making that step from being a relatively healthy, albeit, haunted individual, to realising that one has an illness calls for a redefinition of the self as mentally unstable, if not psychologically challenged.

Trial Commitment

Trial commitment often kicks in at a later stage where unacceptable behavior in the form of self harm (more common in women) and violence (more common in men), for example, sends them along to a recommended psychiatrist. Often, medication only becomes allowed in when, through no fault of their own, the depressed person finds themself in a psychiatric hospital after ending up in Accident and Emergency with an overdose. Alternatively, finding oneself recuperating from a hangover and a painful encounter with some unforgiving wall, or locked up in a police cell again; one is persuaded to see a psychiatrist. It is at this point of sobering confinement that the depressed person may receive their first real diagnoses, which can be both a relief and a shock. Through a regime of treatment in the form of medication and attending a group session with other sufferers, it may be possible to redefine oneself in a supportive environment.

After the treatment package has kicked in and the patient has received all the support they need to help them through a wobbly period, they may be discharged from hospital with their medication and several follow up visits to the psychiatrist or a weekly visit from a Community Psychiatric Nurse (CPN). With the help of their GP or psychiatrist the patient gradually tapers off medication and returns to work, if they have any. With the loss of medical and psychiatric support and the stress of getting back to work, various stress triggers will come into play, creating stress on top of stress in the form of panic attacks and growing anxiety. This transitional period of getting back to normal life can be negotiated successfully, but after a failed or botched attempt the convalescent will go back onto medication and perhaps be on it indefinitely. Depression caused by bereavement or an emotional setback of some kind or in the face of important exams usually responds well to an interim of medication. Here, their efficacy for a presenting short term problem and their subsequent withdrawal is irrefutable. Alternatively, a depressed person may be on medication for some months, even a couple of years, and hit a period of feeling 'better than well' – which is quite common in the summer months. Independently, they reach a decision to give up their medication, as this case history of a young girl in her early 20s illustrates:

I'd been on antidepressants for a couple of years and had been feeling very good. I had a new boyfriend and was doing well in my job and I just thought giving up the tablets was the right thing to do. I skipped doses then dropped them all together and still felt fine. But after a few weeks things began to get me down and irritate me and I thought it was work. Then my boyfriend dumped me – and suddenly I was rock bottom.

The next thing I knew I woke in A&E and they were pumping my stomach because I had taken an overdose. I only vaguely remember taking those pills. Obviously, I had to agree to see the shrink and before I knew it I was sectioned and spent three weeks in a psychiatric hospital...

I'm back on medication now and feel okay again... I have to tell myself that it is dangerous to go off medication too suddenly, if at all...

This case history is not dissimilar to many others. In my hospital working environment there are usually at least four patients on each ward at a time with long term underlying depression. It isn't unusual to have one patient who has taken an overdose on a ward at any given time awaiting psychiatric review. I would say that fifty percent of the patients have stopped medication prior to taking the overdose. I have to point out here that it is not the coming off medication that can trigger off a suicidal state, but that stopping the medication too suddenly can leave one especially vulnerable to mood swings and weakens one's ability to tackle challenging life situations. Life is stressful enough as it is, but for people especially vulnerable to any additional stress, withdrawing from medication too quickly can be the trigger that sends one over the edge.

Conversion

In converting to the medical model, Karp further writes 'Once patients have accepted and internalized rhetoric of biochemical causation they become committed to a process of finding the 'right' medication'.

Finding the right medication is often achieved through a process of trial and error with a hit and miss plethora of symptoms and side effects that can be annoying and unsettling. If the right medication is taken correctly then, hopefully, their benefits will far outweigh their disadvantages. A number of the horror stories that abound, which concern medication withdrawal, happen because drugs are stopped too suddenly or they are not taken for long enough periods.

Some drugs work surprisingly well. Again, I use some of Karp's work to illustrate the 'miracle' of medication, written by a young female graduate:

All I can tell you is, oh my God, you know when you're on the right medication; it was the most incredible thing. And I would say that I had a spiritual experience.

Karp cites a number of case histories that support this where patients who have been haunted and tortured by suicidal destructive thoughts find that this changes with the intervention of medication. A college professor of 50 writes:

...And I started thinking better thoughts, happier thoughts. It was very clear to me that it wasn't the same as being high. Astonishing! It was wonderful... After two weeks... I mean, it was just magical. My life began to change profoundly at that point...

It is interesting that Karp refers to this experience of conversion as tantamount to a 'religious conversion'. Feeling well, feeling yourself, in tune with your innermost centre are all symptoms of a spiritual experience. Incidentally, the root meaning of 'well' is 'whole'. Wholeness is a sense of inner integration with oneself and with all life.

This 'displacement of spiritual longing' as the late psychiatrist, Julian May, intimates in his book, *Addiction and Grace*, does not translate into spiritual experience or union with the Divine because of attachments to the objects of the world that simulate spiritual experience. And this is the nature of addiction: a focused attachment that overrides all other aspirations and sabotages our journey as the snake in the Garden of Eden who tempts us to partake of knowledge rather than truth. Although truth 'can set us free', our attachment to knowledge can enslave us further. As Thomas Merton writes 'There is a natural desire for heaven, for the fruition of God in us'.

And here is the message of the serpent in that Eden experience: 'Anything that makes us feel too good entraps the spirit and makes us slave to repeating the experience.'

Within this drive to be well, is the hungering and pining for a sense of wholeness that can only come into being through union with the Divine, spiritual aspiration and a subduing of the senses that mindlessly attach themselves to any pleasurable experience that make us feel good.

This period of conversion, after the long and protracted stage of resistance and the mental torture that has been endured, may seem like a honeymoon period – the 'ah-ha' experience in the creative process. Any relief from pain whether it be physical pain in the form of an analgesic or mental pain is wonderful. For other people, a holiday may put them in touch with a larger than life experience, or an unexpected romance, a religious retreat or a swim in the sea. A friend of mine experienced this miraculous 'ah-ha' experience when she had some 'spinal touch' treatment on her back which alleviated a long and persistent problem.

Relief from mental anguish is magical.

But as the saying goes; all good things come to an end. The conversion experience falters as shadows emerge from nowhere to cast their pall over the drug's efficacy in the form of disillusionment, and in this case – disenchantment.

Disenchantment

In modern terms, this gradual inefficacy of the medication to continue fulfilling what it was intended to is known as 'poop out'. The medication no longer works as it used to, or doesn't work at all. Although as higher doses may be sought, somehow one never returns to the original 'honeymoon' period.

'Poop- outs' can kick in a year into the treatment, several years after or not at all. This failure in efficacy is not just confined to antidepressants, or solely mental health drugs, but to all drugs in general. Heart medicines, anti-histamines and beta blockers can be effective for a while, but then stop as the physiological system changes. Underlying this is the non permanence of life as Buddhist philosophy so succinctly conveys. There is impermanence in the lifetime relationship with a partner who changes in such a way that we can no longer live together; change within the family matrix of birth and death; the loved friend moves away to another country; the stable job collapses; the promotion we had been waiting for is axed.

Disillusionment and, in this context, disenchantment are part of the journey. Furthermore, this is an integral and crucial part of the journey; because it is not in feeling harmonious and well that sends us searching for deeper meaning. It is in the uncertainty, instability of life that we become hungry for spiritual truth.

At this point medication may be abandoned but, more often than not, with a terminal illness, it is followed like Adriane's thread into a surfeit of other medications which may or may not work. And, perhaps, because the depressed person has experienced an extended period of wellness/wholeness it is even harder to accept the limitations which such an illness imposes on us.

Chapter 7

The Roots of Psychology

Although psychology and psychotherapy are relatively new scientific disciplines, they have emerged from a much older tradition of healing and medicine. This tradition was embedded deep within the matrix of world culture and underpinned the diversity of so called 'primitive' healing techniques. To understand this we need to look at what has now become the mythical tradition of shamanism, wise women and priest status. Basically the shaman was the tribal logos around which the group constellated. The shaman was well known and respected throughout the world from Siberia, to the Inuit communities, the Sami people, the Aborigines to Africa and the North American Indians. Unlike psychology and counseling today, which is fast becoming a popular career choice, very few people wanted to become a shaman. It was a mantle that involved extreme suffering on all levels of being. And yet it was this source of suffering which became the criteria for passage into this realm that involved communication between the spirit world and the realm of the gods.

But usually the shaman was 'called' to take on the role in many different ways throughout their life. This calling often presented itself through bodily dis-ease which became increasingly progressively, more debilitating, until the call was answered and received.

Shamanism could present itself through ancestral lineage or through some disfigurement or incapacity which would make it hard for the person to engage in a normal everyday life. It might even manifest through a depressive illness where the wound of the healer became the means by which the shaman could empathize with others.

The shaman would gain insight into a patient's condition by descending or ascending the 'world tree' and entering upper and lower realms of experiential contact with spirits, gods or demons. Within his shamanic trance he would sometimes voluntarily take on the patient's illness to gain understanding of it and learn from the spirits what needed to be done in order to alleviate the disease. At this level, psyche (mind) and soma (body) were interconnected and were therefore held within the same field of healing. Sickness in the body and mind were inseparable. It was the shaman's task to align the patient with meaning, purpose and values by appeasing the spirits or gods that were looking after his patient's destiny. This alignment became the opening for the patient's future life work.

The shaman was both religious and practical, and within societies shaped around such healers there was no division between religion and science. The shaman's ability to take on their patient's condition still takes place today in both humanistic, transpersonal and psychospiritual therapies. This is true alchemy where the therapist takes on the condition of the client in order to understand it better. He/she 'holds' the condition, allowing the client to step outside the imprisoning restraints of his/her personality and view it with detachment. The therapist literally becomes the change agent. Homeostasis between the clients intrapsychic and interpersonal world occurs as a result of the interaction between therapist and client.

With the introduction of the Descartian-Newton mechanistic model, which shaped the world view in the 17th century, the gods and spirits were steadily replaced by the new god of science. Yet, as Carl Jung asserted; at the point that the gods and spirits were exiled from the Western world, they became internalized in the psyche of the patient instead. These so called 'aberrations' became enlisted under the rapidly emerging labels of neuroses and hysteria. What is denied or repressed is ever striving to come into consciousness and form, or as Roberto Assagioli's famous words suggest: 'What is denied, rules.'

In hindsight, we have the privilege of being able to exact the best in past situations as well as the worst. It is important, now we have consciousness and responsibility, not to polarize to one way of thinking in favor of another. Polarizing towards the scientific medical model or the spiritual model only feeds the split that has formed. With hindsight and the ability to pan out to the greater picture, we can see that both the mechanistic model and the mystical one form two sides of the same picture, just as the two hemispheres of the brain, joined by the corpus colloseum, work together and are, therefore, complementary to each other.

Through this, we can admire the value of Freud's work in psychodynamic psychology and psychoanalysis, in that it formed the ground – the bedrock – of the psychologies which were to follow. Although counseling and psychotherapy may support somebody suffering from depression, they may not alleviate all forms of depression where there is deep clinical disease. And it would be unwise to assume so. However, a therapy such as Cognitive Behavior Therapy (CBT) may prove to be extremely beneficial when used in conjunction with a suitable medication. Medication may stabilize the clinically depressed sufficiently to make counseling or psychotherapy possible. Counseling can support the depressed person in a way that medication cannot and vice versa. I do need to emphasize this from both personal experience and seeing too many people give up their medication in the belief that therapy can replace medication and suffer unpleasant and often dangerous relapses as a result.

Psychodynamic Therapy

It was in the early 1920s when Sigmund Freud emerged on the scene with his psychodynamic theory of the unconscious. In fact, he was purported to have re-invented the unconscious. He also presented his model of the personality which was made up of the *Id, Ego* and *Superego.*

The id, he asserted was unconscious and made up of raw instinctual energies which respond to the *Pleasure Principle* and demand immediate satiation and fulfillment. We can see this in the young infant who cries and screams when it is hungry or uncomfortable. The cry is loud, insistent and demanding and has to be to ensure its survival. Early on, the ego, the organizing centre and locus of human identity, begins to form and adheres to what is known as the *Reality Principle.* The infant begins to differentiate between the 'me' and the 'not me' and perceives himself as distinct from the world around him. Boundaries are created in the initial stage of ego development between the 'me' and the outside world.

At about the age of three, the superego forms. The superego is made up of injunctions and rules that govern our behavior and are externalized through our culture and are often imposed by parental figures. The superego is sometimes known as the morality principle as it holds the boundaries between right and wrong, and acceptable and unacceptable behavior in society.

So the ego is the mediator between the raw impulses of the id and the sobering ones of the superego. The ego, which is created to protect the core of the young vulnerable infant, works hard to make the world a safe place for the developing child. Its central role is to protect and provide stability for the infant, behaving as an outer shell that protects the soft flesh of the crab of the oyster.

Although uncomfortable feelings and memories are repressed or relegated to the unconscious they still drive a lot of our behavior. To continue to protect the vulnerable unformed self, the ego develops various defense mechanisms in the form of displacement, projection, repression and denial. There may be regression to an earlier, less threatening state of development. Until these defense mechanisms are brought to consciousness, we act impulsively and compulsively and are blind to the impact of our behavior on others and the world. We can feel driven without knowing why and experience that life is happening to us rather than being proactive in the world. We are protected from the sense of our own helplessness by acting out various behavior patterns which give us a false sense of autonomy.

Freud's psychodynamic theory underpins many psychotherapeutic practices today and has had a major role in forming the central building block upon which most psychology and psychiatry rest. Psychiatrists such as Assagioli, Jung, Laing and Hillman were all students of Freud and were, for some time, firm adherents of his work.

Despite the criticism Freud received towards his concentration on sexuality, he laid important foundations for the future of psychiatry and psychology, much of which is still used today. In true shamanic style he traveled deep into the unconscious and suffered some sort of breakdown there in service of his work. His objective was to reach the inner being of the human being. He used his love of archaeology, which included excursions to various places like Greece and Egypt, to bring back artifacts, as a rich metaphor for his work with the unconscious! These artifacts were so important to Freud that he refused to leave Nazi occupied Vienna where, because of his Jewish background, his life was endangered until he received assurance that his collection would leave with him.

This lends an endearing quality to his make up that highlights his one-pointedness in fulfilling his life mission. In his later years, when his face was greatly disfigured by innumerable cancer operations on his jaw, he continued to work with patients even though he was still in great pain. The depth of insight that he offered patients into their unconscious processes, both within his own time and in the service of future generations, should never be forgotten.

Although his method can be criticized for its emphasis on analyses, he was emerging from an age where science and mechanistic ways of thinking superseded the mythical and magical ways of being. He was the voice of his time – the zeitgeist for the period.

One of the precepts of Freud's work was that most of our actions and thoughts are driven by the unconscious so we have little control over our lives until, through therapy, they are brought to consciousness. He believed that most of our behavior is a way of alleviating or deflecting what can be unbearable anxiety. Here he advocated love and work as the means through which the human race could achieve some level of happiness within them.

Another of his precepts was *Eros* (the life instinct) and *Thanatos* (the death instinct), which we all carry within us. Freud believed that most of the time we oscillate between the drive for life and love and Thanatos, our destructive impulses. Looking at the amount of people smoking today, when every cigarette packet clearly carries a government health warning, in bold letters: 'smoking can seriously damage your health', we can see we are leaning towards Thanatos. Similarly, many of the things that we enjoy in life and give us pleasure, including the obvious ones of drinking and speed car racing, swimming, deep sea diving, pot holing, rock climbing, evoke thanatos. And perhaps that is why life and death are inseparable. In Tibetan mysticism, learning to die properly is just as important as learning to live properly. This philosophy instructs that unless you can come to terms with your own mortality, Thantaos, then you cannot live properly. This is because, unconsciously, the fear of death eclipses the ability to truly live.

Many people truly only ever feel alive if they are risk taking. By the same token, those who never take risks, feel barely alive. I suppose the answer is to walk the edge between the two. Psychiatrist, Bruno Bettleheim, in his touching biography of Freud, wrote 'We should not see malaise as anything unusual; Goethe said that in seventy-five years he had experienced barely four weeks of being truly at ease.' And it should be remembered here the tremendous value of being able to withstand conflict, frustration and tension in service of building a healthy ego.

Freudian Therapy and Transference

The main drive behind the therapeutic relationship is based on transference. This is a process where the client transfers previous significant parental and authoritarian figures onto the therapist and interacts with the positive or negative transference. Through maintaining the transference, past figures that may have had a negative influence on the client as a child, can be faced and explored. When this process has become conscious to the client, the therapist can invite dialogue between them through role-playing. By opening up awareness of how the client is 'driven' by powerful parental injunctions that have outlived their usefulness, the sources of anxiety, depression and discomforted are unraveled and, ideally, the client experiences a greater sense of autonomy. The therapist literally makes himself a blank screen so that transference is possible; understanding that any anger, sadness and ambivalence directed towards him is not personal but rather through displaced feelings from some past figure/object. Working with a blank screen is not a comfortable or easy process although valuable insights may be gained.

The Freudian therapist can seem impassive, clinical and intellectual without a great deal of empathy. The theory behind depression (in Freud's day referred to as melancholia) is that it is mourning for a lost object which can take the form of lost libido or a significant other. In a relationship this may be the presumed loss of a mother's love at the birth of a new sibling or the loss of a loved partner or friend. But underlying this is anger at the loss which becomes internalized and directed at oneself instead of at the other.

Where ambivalence, shame and guilt have become internalized and directed at oneself in the form of depression, Freudian therapy is helpful in enabling one to find a handle on reactive depression based on internalized repressed memories. Having said this, this isn't for everyone and there is no harm in having a couple of initial sessions to see whether this is helpful or not.

Psychoanalyses in Service of Depression
The Freudian analyst is unlikely to be interested in exploring the spiritual aspect of the client's symptom. He will be much more interested in mining the depths of the unconscious for signs of trauma, abuse and splitting within the developmental framework of childhood. Relationships with parents and siblings and other important family members will be explored. Contextualizing depression within a spiritual or transpersonal framework may be seen as a way of denying or repressing historical material that is too painful to deal with. Any 'peak experience' will be translated on a personality level as developing a sense of omnipotence, autonomy and self worth which wasn't allowed to be expressed during childhood. The development of self-confidence and self-will are seen as demonstrations of a strengthening ego. Both developmental regression and progression are enacted in service of the ego, rather than translated on a higher octave in service of the Self. The downside of this is that valuable transpersonal experiences may be acted out on a personality level which can give rise to inflation and arrogance rather than harnessing the humility that is needed to integrate them.

Despite this, however, psychoanalyses is excellent in building emotional and psychological ground and enabling one to face long repressed memories that serve to hinder personality development rather than free one to move forward. In soul development the groundwork we carry out on the personality level is absolutely crucial in creating a strong enough container to hold the insights of the Self.

Cognitive Behavior Therapy

CBT has been cited as the leading therapy used in the treatment of depression in the States. It has proven to be especially effective in treating young people, from children to teenagers, who suffer from depression. A rising percentage of one in twenty teenagers develops mental health disorders such as depression where suicidal thoughts are involved. Since depression spirals rapidly upwards in females at adolescence, a gender based cognitive program was devised to work with these troubled teenagers. The results were good with an impressive eighty percent success rate.

Where behaviorism has provided insight into the importance of the environment affecting behavior, CBT emphasized the effect of thinking (cognition) upon emotions and action (behavior). CBT theorists work on the principle that it wasn't the actual event (stimulus) that elicited a negative or positive response but our reaction to it.

Cognitive Behavior Therapy was developed in the 1950s and 1960s by American psychiatrists, Albert Ellis and Aaron Beck. Ellis, the highly controversial founder, began to apply the foundation of this technique when he was 19 to situations that he found highly challenging and anxiety provoking. He analyzed that there was a powerful connection between thoughts, feelings and behavior; that habitual recurrent thoughts would elicit feelings of aversion which would ultimately impact on behavior. By challenging these thoughts he began to slowly create new thoughts patterns which had a positive feedback loop into associative behavior.

Internal Dialogue
Aaron T Beck had come to notice that during his analytical

sessions his clients had an 'internal dialogue' running in their minds all the time. For example, the client would be simultaneously thinking, 'I wonder if he's irritated with me,' or 'I bet he thinks I'm an idiot.' And later on there may be secondary thoughts; 'I bet I'm making him tired and he can't wait to get rid of me.' These repetitive compulsive thoughts have a direct effect on the feelings and behavior of the client. He referred to these thoughts as 'automatic' thoughts. He believed that the link between thoughts and feelings was crucial to the wellbeing of the client. He realized that very few people were aware of this internal dialogue and he saw that bringing awareness of this to his clients was crucial in their work together. As his clients learnt to identify these self-critical thoughts and reported them, they began to gain more control over their moods as the thoughts were rarely helpful. This was what he termed the cognitive approach.

Irrational Thoughts and Beliefs
He also noticed that many of his clients had repetitive irrational thoughts which greatly undermined their perception of life and, furthermore, created a maintaining self-fulfilling cycle of failure and low self-esteem. Some of these irrational thoughts were:

I cannot be happy unless everyone likes me.
If I do what is expected of me, my life will be wonderful.
Bad things don't happen to good people.
Good things don't happen to bad people.
In the end, bad people will always get punished.
If I am intelligent (or work hard), I will be successful.

These patterns of thinking develop into mindsets that are perceived as reality. Work with a cognitive therapist will examine these irrational thoughts and question their validity and use in the here and now.

CBT is a highly effective technique for re-structuring the way we think using mental imagery, relaxation and journal keeping, all of which facilitate a growing awareness of the destructive thoughts patterns we get enmeshed in. This represents the cognitive aspect. The behavioral aspect is changed by locating the behaviors, both overt and covert, in our repetitive thoughts towards an event and behaving differently in response to eliciting a changed perspective. For example, a woman who was obsessive about keeping her house clean, used to get upset when her friends and visitors left tread marks all over her carpet. A CBT therapist reframed this for her by remarking 'Isn't it wonderful that you should be loved and cared for by so many people – that so many friends and relations want to take the time and energy to visit you.' The woman responded affirmatively, adding that she had never looked at it like that before. As a result, she was able to look forward to her social visits rather than seeing them as a hindrance. Basically, the stimulus hadn't changed, but her reaction to it had.

The efficacy in CBT is in the active working relationship between client and therapist. CBT recognizes that consciousness and insight into faulty thought patterns are not enough to dispel them and so homework is set for the intervening time between the next meetings. This consists of maintaining a journal, achievable targets and self-evaluation. All this is instrumental in forging new neural pathways in the brain, and there is evidence-based proof of this in brain scans that reveal significant changes that underpin this.

Really CBT is nothing new, as reframing our thinking in order to access a more creative and potentially positive way of perceiving the world has been practiced by mystics and philosophers throughout history, from Plato and Epicurus to Joel Goldsmith, Catherine Pounder, Ernest Holmes, Norman Vincent Peale and Louise Hay. None of these people started out with a silver spoon in their mouth. Quite the contrary, in fact, because each of them discovered that their thoughts had a direct effect on their life so they resolved to gain some mastery over their thinking process and gradually changed their life.

I worked as editor and writer for a number of years for the journal, *Science of Thought Review*. The pioneer was Henry Thomas Hamblin who founded the magazine in the 1920s which was to influence the minds of many during the two world wars. He wrote popular publications such as, *Right Thinking, The Power of Thought, Within You is the Power, Life without Strain* and *Divine Adjustment*. All of these, plus the monthly magazine, now called *New Vision*, has survived him by nearly fifty years. I remember his motto was 'Change your thoughts and change your life.' Hamblin, himself, as a young man, suffered from a near crippling lack of self-esteem and faith in himself. It was this fundamental lack of inner confidence and trust in life which was to become the pivotal point in his fashioning what was to later become his purpose and lifework. This so cogently illustrates how it is the weaknesses within us that we rally against which have the potential to become our strengths. Our weaknesses are our jewels waiting to be discovered when we accept them.

Present and Future

Although CBT accepts that some understanding of one's personal history can identify how our negative attitude came into being, it does not focus on working with the past history as many therapies do. Since behavior and thinking is learned from faulty social conditions, new ways of behaving and thinking are drawn up by the therapist. Both the therapist and client agree on what the problems are, together with what they want to eliminate and develop. Agreed goals are drawn up within a daily program of actively working to meet the targets. It has been found that new cognitive pathways in the brain are formed by replacing negative and irrational beliefs with more realistic positive ones. The client works at their own speed and returns to the therapist each week to report back progress and pick up on any difficulties they may have encountered. On average the client will need 12-16 sessions and when they are both happy with the way the treatment is progressing, agree to meet up once a month or several months after.

CBT in Service of Depression

In the 1970s, many psychologists began writing about cognitive aspects of depression, identifying different cognitive components that affected depression, and developing cognitive interventions to treat depression. Further theory and research produced evidence that cognitive therapy was not only an effective tool in the treatment of negative mental states, but was possibly the most successful intervention strategy for treating depression. Since the 1970s, the use of cognitive therapy with depression has increased tremendously, and the number of psychologists using cognitive therapy approaches for the treatment of all psychological problems has also grown. Because of CBT's focus on left brain activity in talking, reading and writing, this has a pacifying effect on the amygdala which is renowned for sending out negative messages. Talking and thinking about emotions brings consciousness to them so that we have some control over them. Elevating emotions and feelings to a cortical level helps tone down the signals that give rise to depression. In this way, CBT appears to be the number one strategy for many types of depression. But it must also be remembered that all psychotherapy has cognitive components. One of the major differences between cognitive therapy and other therapeutic approaches is the treatment interventions used to change human cognitive experiences.

Cognitive behavior therapy is a well-established therapy and is non-invasive in that little attention is given to the past and the unconscious. It focuses on a series of tangible steps of progress which can be modified to suits the client's needs. The client has control over the sessions and how fast they want to travel.

Buddha as the 'first Cognitive Behavior Therapist'
John Winston Bush PHD, Executive Director of New York Institute for Cognitive Therapies in Brooklyn, describes Buddha as being the first 'cognitive behavior therapist'. As his teaching involved the alleviation of suffering, he developed a system of 'being mindful' by observing the thoughts and focusing on the breathing. Like cognitive therapy, Buddha believed that it wasn't the actual events that caused the suffering, but our reaction and attachment to the event that was the problem. Buddha's teaching was to live in the present and not to get trapped in the past. As in Buddhism, which focuses on mindfulness and relaxation techniques through breathing and meditation, CBT coaches the client in staying in the present and developing awareness of thoughts and various relaxation techniques which call upon creative imagery.

Humanistic Counseling
Although humanistic psychology was said to emerge in the 1950s, its roots are embedded in the older tradition of the healer/shaman, who treated the whole person rather than the parts. The main founder here was American psychologist, Abraham Maslow, the 'spiritual father' of humanistic psychology. It is interesting that Maslow started out as an enthusiastic behaviorist but became increasingly disillusioned by its reductive approach, where real people ceased to be people. Latterly, he became deeply critical of the somewhat reductionist and mechanistic psychologies of psychoanalysis and behaviorism. He concentrated on looking at the whole person, rather than the parts. While behaviorism and psychoanalyses focused on what was wrong with the client, Maslow focused on the positive aspects of the personality like a basic goodness and creativity. He believed these positive aspects were inherent in all individuals; although they may have gone underground through trauma, they could be coaxed into the foreground through

acceptance and trust.

Maslow devised a hierarchy of needs that had to be attained before self-actualisation could occur. This hierarchy of needs worked from the bottom up from physiological needs, security needs, and social needs to ego needs. The individual could gain greater autonomy and become creative through having their basic needs met. We all know that when we enter a group situation we have an inherent need to feel safe, to belong.

Maslow's Pyramid

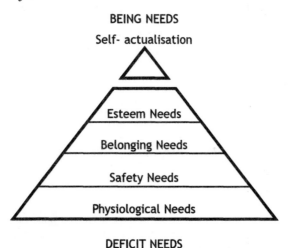

BEING NEEDS

Self- actualisation

Esteem Needs

Belonging Needs

Safety Needs

Physiological Needs

DEFICIT NEEDS

Self-actualization is the point where people become fully functional and able to realize their potential. Self-actualization is the basic force that drives the person forward. When a person is achieving their potential, they have what Maslow termed as a 'peak experience'. Self-actualization is the desire and drive to becoming everything we are capable of becoming.

Maslow believed that we should study and cultivate peak experiences as a way of providing a route to achieve personal growth, integration and fulfillment. Peak experiences are unifying and ego-transcending, bringing a sense of purpose to the individual and a sense of integration. Individuals most likely to have peak experiences are self-actualized, mature, healthy, and self-fulfilled. All individuals are capable of peak experiences; those who do not have them somehow repress or deny them.

Maslow carried out an in-depth study of self-actualizers throughout history and within contemporary society. He identified a number of characteristics they all had.

- Acceptance of themselves and others
- More efficiency in perceiving reality
- More spontaneity in their relationships
- A tendency to focus on the solutions to problems rather than the problems themselves.
- An autonomy from cultural influences and societal injunctions
- A capacity for transcendence/intense mystical experiences
- A deep identification with humanity with empathy
- A sense of humor
- An ability to be creative

Transpersonal Psychology

All transpersonal psychologies fully embrace the need for a good grounding in healthy ego development. Unless essential goalposts are met in ego development through healthy mirroring there will be too much temptation to resort to spiritual flight in order to feel special or important. I explore these milestones which challenge the spiritual pathway further on in this work, alongside the levels of psychological development which need to be negotiated before the transpersonal level can be integrated within the psyche (see Part III). The transpersonal theorists understood the importance of building a healthy ego in order to ground the insights that were accessible from the superconscious. The problem is not so much in believing that we are primarily a spiritual being living in a physical body, but in *understanding* one's psychological strength and weaknesses enough to deal with this insight. For example, it wasn't by chance that in the Jewish mystical tradition of the Kabbalah, students were not accepted into the study of the Tree of Life until they were 40 or were at least married. This was so that the potential student's insight could be properly grounded in the world and that they had built up a strong enough sense of self through facing the rigors of life. Conscious dedication to the spiritual path is never an easy choice, although it may be seen as a means of escape.

Although Carl Jung, Roberto Assagioli, Charles Tart, Stanislav Groff and Ken Wilber have become richly associated with developing transpersonal psychology, Maslow and his work on self-actualization and peak experiences was one of the original pioneers.

Additionally, Charles Tart, professor of psychiatry at the university of California and lecturer in psychology at Stanford University, has been one of the leading researchers and proponents in transpersonal psychology. He defines transpersonal psychology as going beyond the ego which represents the reality principle. Good at posing key questions which open up awareness he asks 'Why would anyone want to go beyond the ego if this is our link with reality? Is it to escape the confines of a reality that has become unbearable or to look for further meaning?'

He believed that the fundamental preoccupation for those interested in transpersonal experiences was a need to inject a new sense of purpose into their lives; one that would redefine the meaning of their life experience.

Under the heading of 'transpersonal experience' are altered states of consciousness (ASC), out of the body experiences (OBEs), peak experience, unidentified flying object encounters (UFOs) and spontaneous healing. All these impact on the psyche in such a way that there is a profound change in inner values and perspective.

Deep values, he perceived, really come from an intense

personal experience. As a result one's sense of purpose is activated, conferring greater meaning and depth to life. Usually the founders of a particular religion or spiritual faith have experienced some intense personal contact with a spiritual insight or truth in the form of a vision or teaching. This experience is energetic and attracts others to itself. But as time passes, and the magnetism that initially drew people to the 'truth' becomes watered down, the sense of aliveness that animated the work diminishes. In time, the rational scientific mind dismisses it as 'poppycock': a set of superstitions that have outlived their usefulness. Unless a spiritual insight initiates a technology of practice for its followers to carry out, in the form of meditation, prayer and visualization, the religion or truth cannot sustain itself. Practice is as important as the original core teaching. It sustains the insight and strengthens the connection. This is true for all the major religions which firmly encourage diligent and regular practice.

One of Charles Tart's preoccupations was to build bridges between science and religion rather than maintain the splits. He highlights the need for both scientists and mystics to smooth the split that separates the two by fostering a sense of humility. Humility counteracts the danger of arrogance that arises in both the mystic, the one who has had the transpersonal experience and the scientist who defends himself strongly against anything that can threaten his mindset. Humility, he believed, opens the door to true dialogue between the two, whereas arrogance keeps the door locked and barred. He writes:

The conflict is between second rate science and second rate mystics, between dogmatic people... When people become psychologically attached to their beliefs though, they become defensive, and feel the need to attack other people's beliefs and conflict arises.

Unless there is openness to talking through one's insights rather than rushing to convert others, then the transpersonal experience cannot be properly integrated. That is why it is so essential to have grounding in early ego development, or else one identifies with the transpersonal experience and become inflated, thinking 'they are the one'. This is no good to anyone and can be dangerous if the experience becomes enmeshed with the ego. No transpersonal experience, however profound, can take the place of good grounding and healthy ego development.

Jungian Analytical Therapy

In many ways, Carl Jung has become the icon of a mystical psychologist for the New Age. Although Jung understood the need to develop a spiritual connection with life, he did not become too preoccupied himself with developing along these lines. He resisted being labeled a 'mystic' by developing a strong outer persona that applied a scientific context to his life and work. By his own definition he looked upon himself as 'an empiricist who moved within the limits of a natural empirical science'. Jung, like Assagioli, understood the importance of maintaining an infallible scientific context to his work in order to gain respect and credibility from a public that was only too ready to overturn psychology as hogwash. Only his close friends and colleagues saw another deeper side to Jung that embraced a more spiritual philosophy. But it was one that had revealed itself to him slowly, as having a father who was a parson and had no desire to share his beliefs with his questing son, had turned him against religion with its rigidity and narrow confines. In fact, Jung described himself an agnostic. And yet, as his rich autobiography reveals he was an inherently spiritual man. Although greatly reluctant to set down details of his life, he knew that at the time of writing it, he was approaching the end of his life and this is what people wanted. He once described the writing of it as 'purgatory' and said about his spiritual life:

I have guarded this material all my life, and have never wanted it exposed to the world... I have suffered enough from incomprehension and from the isolation one falls into when one says things that people do not understand.

The Collective Unconscious

Like Freud, Jung had a passion for exploring the unconscious and that was probably what united them in the beginning and made Freud believe that the young Carl Jung could become his successor. But Jung's explorations moved beyond the personal unconscious into what he referred to as the 'collective unconscious'. While the personal unconscious was a repository of everything the individual had experienced but may not be conscious of at the time, the collective unconscious was there from the beginning. It was as if modern man came into form bearing ancestral memories of his past, just as the shamans had maintained. The unconscious, therefore, wasn't dependent on experience; it seemed to exist within a large racial pool from which people could draw. Within this collective reservoir Jung differentiated instincts and archetypes which in themselves were primordial blueprints and thought forms of humanity. Jung also embraced the world of symbols and believed that these were potent representations of the psyche, the real self.

If Freud described dreams as being the royal road to the unconscious, Jung exemplified this in his work. He believed that the more attention one paid to dreams, the more accessible they became. He recommended that anyone interested in understanding themselves better should begin by keeping a journal by their bed and immediately assigning the memory of a dream to paper on waking. Over a period of weeks, dreams would become more distinct and in time, one would be able to see several dreams running simultaneously, installment by installment.

My personal experience verifies this when I kept a dream diary for several years. Sometimes what was going on in my unconscious was hugely more fascinating and exciting than my daily life! Somehow, the act of committing my dreams to paper grounded them and made them distinctly more tangible than before I had bothered writing them down.

The Shadow

Although Jung was very grateful to Freud for his insight and work on neuroses, rather than seeing this in a wholly negative light, as a result of repressed traumatic memories, he contended that neuroses was essentially creative; something was struggling to right itself in the individual. Above all, he saw that nothing was really cut and dried. Everything was in a state of process and becoming. Being able to facilitate and encourage that process became an integral non-invasive core of his work.

One of Jung's major contributions to the field of psychology was the naming of the shadow which is the dark undifferentiated part of us that grows alongside the ego. Jung sometimes referred to this as the 'dark brother' or 'dark angel'. Although absent in the young child, the shadow continues to grow throughout the child's developmental process. His premise was to always acknowledge the presence of one's shadow or else we project it onto others. The 'projected' shadow underpins ethnic cleansing and prejudice where the 'other', in the form of the enemy, is seen to hold the unacknowledged dross of the prosecutor. Jung firmly believed that the more the undifferentiated part of us is repressed or denied, the stronger grows the shadow.

The shadow, as we know from out own inner experience, is deeply resistant to being found out. Its ways are cunning and devious and this is more so in a culture such as ours where there are such well-defined demarcations between good and bad, acceptable and unacceptable. The more we exile our shadow on both a personal and collective level, the more we meet it in each other. The only way we can tame our shadow is through acceptance and love. Bringing the shadow to light divests the dark twin of its power as the troll in the light of day loses its menace and hold over us. Assagioli cited cogently in his teaching 'Whatever is denied rules'. When we are able to accept and fully embrace the dark unrefined dross of our deepest self, we have a greater chance of accepting it in those who 'trespass against us'. The temptation that haunts us the most is our obsession with exiling it and only presenting the 'good' side of ourselves.

As children we have a healthy obsession to explore and unearth the dark and mysterious. In all the fairy tales the dark heroes and heroines are unmasked (as in the jealousy of Cinderella's step sisters) and so divested of their power. In Snow White, the wicked queen poisoned the sleeping princess through jealousy, but always the opportunity for redemption is at play. The poisoned apple that looked so tempting can be used as a metaphor for materialism which robs us of our consciousness and sends us into a consensual trance.

In the new-age movement there is a strong drive to only show the good parts of ourselves, to seem to be wise, inviolate and all knowledgeable. But underneath this striving to be seen this way is the antithesis of this: the insecure and weak part which is avoiding being unmasked and yet longing to be seen and accepted. How easily we forget that the very things that endear us to others are the seemingly unlovable unacceptable parts!

Individuation

Jung referred to the process of becoming one's true self as individuation. His work and teaching is concerned with the false persona which we learn to develop as a mask to survive in the world and allowing the true self to shine through. Individuation is a process of becoming self-aware to the ways in which we betray and hide our true self and becoming who we really are.

It was after a very painful split with Freud, who had in many ways become his mentor and support, when Jung underwent a mental breakdown that was to extend over three years. In this time Jung felt overwhelmed by the unconscious content flooding his life and felt that he was becoming psychotic. He believed that had it not been for his family and work with his patients, he would have been sucked right into the abyss, never to emerge again. Within this period he underwent a deep inner initiation which he described as being akin to the 'Dark Night of the Soul' or the shaman's journey into the underworld (see Chapter11). While he was undergoing this rigorous descent he felt exiled from the outside world and his work lost popularity and the world labeled him as a mystic, a term he rebelled against.

In retrospect, Jung believed that this descent into the unconscious offered him a wealth of invaluable insights into the lives of his patients. He contended that knowledge accessed from these deep levels was to become a rich source of wisdom throughout his life. Jung firmly believed that an analyst could only heal and understand a patient from a point of wounding himself. He wrote, to this affect, 'In the end, only the wounded physician heals and even he, in the last analyses, cannot heal beyond the extent to which he has healed himself'. In a very real sense, Jung had undergone an underworld initiation and had emerged as a healer through his own wounds.

Alcoholism as a Cry for Deeper Meaning
Jung's work and sheer magnetism was to have a wide and far - reaching influence among both his contemporaries and the general public in his own time. He was contacted by a Catholic Mother Prioress of a contemplative order who told him what a great influence his writings had on her community as she wrote of her sense of isolation in the world; isolation which Jung understood only too well as he felt there were few who really understood him.

He was also to receive a communication from William Wilson, known as 'Bill W', who co-founded Alcoholics Anonymous, acknowledging how Jung's remarks to a chronically alcoholic patient had been instrumental in Bill's own conversion, cure and in beginning the foundation of Alcoholics Anonymous in 1934. Jung's words of advice to this alcoholic were '…that his situation was hopeless unless he could become the subject of a spiritual or religious experience, in short a genuine conversion'. Bill W touchingly conveyed that many of his AA members were students of his writings. He wrote 'Because of your conviction that man is something more than intellect, emotion and two dollars worth of chemicals, you have especially endeared yourself to us.'

Jung wrote back about the craving for alcohol, expressing it 'as a symptom, on a low level, of the spiritual thirst of our being, longing for wholeness, expressed in medieval language: the union with God… You see 'alcohol' in Latin is *spiritus*, and you use the same word for the highest religious experience as well as for the most depraving poison.'

Jung's insights around alcoholism, masquerading as a call to greater meaning, is especially relevant today where alcohol in our culture is cheap and so readily available on a 24/7 basis. Current statistics reveal that alcohol fuelled behavior has risen by twenty percent in the last five years among young people. As is so often demonstrated throughout this work and other books on depression, many depressives self-medicate with alcohol and other substances in order to alleviate their inner sense of darkness. Certainly amongst the young is the need to find connection with a deeper sense of purpose that was once expressed through the lost rites of passage.

Jung and Depression
Jung understood depression to be a natural response of the self to the loss of soul in the world, and that it served the purpose of allowing the depressed person to go through a period of self-reflection and self analyses. Like alcoholism, he saw that depression was a call to greater meaning. Depression allowed

one to re-evaluate their role and purpose in life and, where they had betrayed their soul, to rectify this and get back on track. He didn't so much see depression as pathological, but is the soul's intention to right itself. He believed depression to be in evidence where the person has had to fall short of being their true self and developed a false sense of self which fed into feelings of betrayal. Through analyzing the dreams and historical background of his patients he was able to locate, in many cases, where the depression found its roots. The inclusion of a letter here that Jung wrote to a patient, who had contacted him over his depression, gives some insights into Jung's thoughts on the subject:

Dear N.,

I am sorry you are so miserable. Depression means literally being forced downwards. This can happen even when you don't consciously have any feeling at all of being 'on top'! So I wouldn't dismiss this hypothesis out of hand. If I had to live in a foreign country, I would seek out one or two people who seemed amiable and would make myself useful to them, so that libido came to me from outside, even though in a somewhat primitive form, say of a dog wagging its tail. I would raise animals and plants and find joy in their thriving. I would surround myself with beauty – no matter how primitive and artless – objects, colours, sounds. I would eat and drink well. When the darkness grows denser, I would penetrate to its very core and ground, and I would wrestle with the dark angel until he dislocated my hip. For he is also the light and the blue sky which he withholds from me.

Anyway that is what I would do. But for you too there is an instinct either to back out of it or to go down to the depths. But no half-measures or half-heartedness.

Post Jungians and Creative Depression

You do a disservice to yourself when you treat your feelings of despair and emptiness as deviations from the normal and healthy life you idealize.
Thomas Moore

Mary Esther Harding, a Jungian therapist, writes on the value and meaning of depression, describing it as a lack of libido, where energy vanishes into the unconscious because its outward flow has been frustrated. Something is impeding its flow. She describes this as being very different to the first where regression is involved. In the second case something is demanding our attention. She refers to this as *creative depression* where the person is being invited to find out what is struggling to be born. This may be in the form of a painting, piece of writing, project or new idea. It is, effectively, mining the depths for gold light of consciousness. Very often, before something is born there is depression, similar to the broodiness a parent may experience before deciding to have a child. Once the creative act is engaged in, the depression disappears (see Chapter 14).

Jung and Assagioli

Assagioli, the founder of Psychosynthesis psychology (see Chapter 8), believed that out of all the methods of counseling and psychology, Jung's work came closest to his own and was in substantial agreement with his goals. The differences lay in the techniques themselves. He admitted that he had used Jung's 'Collective Unconscious' in his famous egg diagram on levels of consciousness and commended him highly for his emphasis of mankind's need to harness spiritual values. Like Assagioli, Jung railed against psychology's obsession with relegating most conditions to pathology and jumping to find a label for every conceivable psychological behavior. This was a legacy from psychodynamic psychology and still exists today.

In all, Assagioli had a great respect for Jung whom he described as a 'courageous and brilliant pioneer who opened up new paths and gave new dimensions in the human mind.' Assagioli said that although Jung assigned the intuition as one of the primary psychological functions, he was disappointed that he didn't assign more work to the creative imagination which is one of the building blocks of psychosynthesis. This is demonstrated by the enlisting of the active imagination in achieving synthesis between opposing forces within the personality. Despite this, Assagioli believed that Jung's lifework favored synthesis over analyses.

Both psychiatrists were in agreement over the use of symbols and although Jung postulates that messages originated from the unconscious to the person, Assagioli went further in additionally assigning them to the 'superconscious'. The major difference between Jung and Assagioli's work was how each viewed the Self. Jung regarded the Self as a psychological archetypal concept; it was an intermediate point where the conscious and unconscious came together. By contrast, Assagioli believed the Self to be a 'living reality'.

It is easy to feel overwhelmed today by the diversity of clinical practice available, but I hope I have made it more accessible. Where depression has originated from traumatic historical issues, certainly the psychodynamic model will be invaluable in sourcing areas of deep conflict and neuroses. I have known people who have, because of their spiritual background, followed one of the transpersonal therapies for a while then, several years later when difficulties have re-emerged through a natural regression, begun psychodynamic therapy which has proved every bit as helpful at transpersonal therapy. All of these therapies have a role to play, even behaviorism out of which cognitive therapy has evolved. And needless to say the psychology, whatever it embraces, is only as good as the counselor or psychotherapist who embodies it. Generally, if you trust your feelings, you will know from the initial meeting with the therapist whether their technique or they themselves are right for you. Most therapists offer an introductory session free of charge where you can find out about meeting goals and drawing up a plan of progress.

Chapter 8

My Journey into Psychosynthesis

Out of all the psychotherapeutic techniques I have studied and tried, I have found psychosynthesis to be one of the most effective in treating depression. And this is mainly due to its inclusion of the psychospiritual element. The main obstacle I encountered was the over zealous attitude of some of my fellow students who believed that psychosynthesis should give me the insight to cure myself. I too shared this disappointment and was left with feelings of failure and really my chapter on *How to be with someone who is Depressed* was a result of this deficit in understanding that I encountered. Thankfully, the tutors and therapists I encountered throughout the training were empathic with the depths of my anguish and fully embraced the teaching that suffering has meaning when I could find no meaning in my suffering. Certainly the teaching of the seminar, *The Meaning of Suffering*, in the fourth year of my training, enabled me to reframe my attitudes to depression. It also relieved me of the shame that I carried with me around not being able to cure what seemed to be an intractable condition. Ironically, the acceptance of my depression has been my therapeutic journey.

The training of a therapist is thorough, taking place over a period of four years, and most important of all, the teaching embraces all levels of psychospiritual development, from the ground upwards. In this chapter I am not advocating that psychosynthesis is the 'right' and 'only' way to treat depression, but it is a way that has worked for me as someone who values the spiritual as well as the psychological and biological components of depression. More than anything it holds that crucial and invisible 'field' open to communication with the Self. This alone, I have found has a tangible effect on depression.

By the time I was 20 I accepted that I regularly underwent a creative darkness that was cyclical, usually beginning in the fall and lifting some time in the late spring. I still found it hard to accept that I had a depressive illness. My belief system embraced a new-age spirituality that looked upon growth and suffering as, at its worst, redemptive and karmic, and at its best a preparation for being an enlightened soul. Again I came across the 'Dark Night of the Soul'. I found people reacted to my depression in one of two ways, they either wanted to fix me with anything from Bach flower remedies to a multitude of different healing techniques or past life regressions, or they said I was obviously a 'special soul' to take on such a burden of suffering. What I internalized in the feedback I met was that depression was shameful and I had obviously done something very bad in a past life. Fortunately, I was to meet Tony, my partner, a man I stayed with for sixteen years. He didn't try to fix my depression as this had run in his family too, but supported me in the way I chose to handle it. He too had inherited some of the descents into blackness from his ancestry and we could support each other. His sense of humor matched mine. Ironically, I have found, the most depressed people can have a delightful and witty humor. My dear uncle was no exception to this and no one who knew his outgoing zany personality would ever believe that a world of terrifying darkness and pain lay behind his cheerful persona – a world that took him to suicide.

While I was with Tony, and too ill to work in the outside world, I developed my creative abilities, by first writing for the romance market in the form of four hundred short stories, then later writing articles for various health magazines. I found I could work creatively with my depression, by writing poetry which found its market in a commercial way and writing for various spirituality-based magazines. Also I was to find a great source of strength from a healing, spiritually-based organization in the form of the White Eagle Lodge. Just before making contact with the leaders of the Stockport Lodge in the 1980s, I had a vision of a shining figure entering my room and taking the darkness from me, so that the months of winter depression left me.

As the years passed, my descents into darkness lasted progressively longer and were more debilitating, driving me to the edge of suicide more times than I can remember. But I put this down to a lowered tolerance of pain. Additionally, I noticed that my periods of being exuberant, when I emerged from the depressive cycle, were not so long or as intense either.

Through my twenties and mid thirties I diligently held to the 'creative darkness' model. This was the only way I could live with the shame of having a condition that seemed self- indulgent when I believed there were so many more pressing problems in the world. I received various types of healing, none of which seemed to shift the condition for any length of time, if at all. Although I have to say that the most effective treatment I had tried, up until then, was a homeopathic one. I had almost instant relief after a few hours which were to last over three or four months, but then when I dropped down into the darkness again, we couldn't find another remedy which worked so efficaciously. These 'hit' and 'miss' treatments are very common, not just for depression, but other illnesses too.

Briefly, I tried the psychological model which held that a lot of my depression and anguish was inverted anger and rage at suffering various forms of psychic, emotional and sexual abuse throughout my early childhood years. If I could somehow cathart all this anger and rage, I would be free to move on. Here, I encountered the 'wounded child' philosophy with whom, through visualization exercises, I needed to enter dialogue with and listen to her story. For a while, I attended an Adult Children's support group where people of all ages were in touch with their inner child and were able to get in touch with their anger, tears, and sense of fun again. After a few months, I began to feel restless, stuck and uncomfortable. It seemed that the weakness in this model of thought was that people regressed to childish rather than childlike ways. There was the temptation to blame relationship and authority problems onto one's early history, without harnessing the necessary insights and strength of character to move forward in life again. There was a reluctance to take personal responsibility, to move beyond blame. It was as if when people found their historical wound they collapsed into it; re-wounding themselves over and over. At this level of consciousness there was no hope of redemption or healing through forgiveness. The group which should have been supportive was binding. The humility that needed to be in place for transformation and healing to take place was eclipsed by pride and self-righteousness. As a result, the consciousness of the group very often polarized towards a tribal one where family history was reenacted in the group. This was basically self-fulfilling and narcissistic where projections were acted out amongst group members which could be raw and threatening. As a result, the humanitarian values which were held as part of the group vision went underground if no one was strong enough to hold them. Rather than sacrifice 'deep belonging' needs, the established group members would compromise their individual ideals in order to reach a group consensus and as a result the newer more idealistic members left. Having said all this, although many of my experiences were negative around this group, I am very grateful for the insight that this has given me into group dynamics. I also met several lovely people, one of whom was herself training to be a psychosynthesis counselor. I believe the principles of the Adult Children's groups, which have emerged from the AA philosophy, to be sound, but group dynamics are extremely powerful and when unconscious material is being re-enacted in the group, it can seriously undermine the group vision. Since the groups are run voluntarily, both in a rotating leadership role and financial contributions, these principles cannot always be maintained.

Fortunately, I persisted with the psychological model. At least long enough to come across a very good counselor who acknowledged the gravity of my personal history, but was able to place the psychological model alongside the spiritual and medical model. He had a sister who was an artist and suffered very similar periods of cyclical depression and exuberance. She had been diagnosed as being bipolar and he suggested that I get this checked out too as it was treatable. To both his own surprise and my own he strongly recommended that I see a doctor or psychiatrist to see whether I needed lithium, a mood stabilizing drug used in the treatment of bipolar disorder.

The idea that I might be suffering from manic depression as it was then called, came with mixed feelings of relief and despair. I felt relief that I suffered from an authentic condition which warranted medical treatment that could ease the level of suffering, and despair that I was stuck with this condition for life as part of a chemical glitch. But most important of all was the fact that my therapist was a psychosynthesis counselor. This was a path I would follow over the next seven years and would eventually lead me into the training program.

Psychiatrist, Mountaineer and Mystic

In order to reach an understanding of psychosynthesis it is important to have some insight into the man responsible for its conception. Roberto Assagioli was born in Venice in 1888. His mother was a Jew and a Theosophist which must have provided him with a preliminary grounding into the importance of the spiritual life. Additionally, he held a great fondness for both Dante Alighieri and his classic work, *The Divine Comedy*, which was taught in schools throughout Italy. Assagioli identified fully with the 13th century poet who was imprisoned and exiled from Florence, his homeland, for the last twenty years of his life. Assagioli's own life was endangered as a Jew during the Second World War and he too was imprisoned and exiled for a period for his political beliefs. He saw *The Divine Comedy* as a complete metaphor for the spiritual journey and, indeed, referred to it as 'a wonderful picture of a complete psychosynthesis'. He equated the descent into the personality depths as *Hell*, or the abyss, and then the aspiration towards transforming the lower aspects of the personality as *Purgatory*, and finally the union with the Self as *Paradise.*

Despite his early coaching in esoteric matters, Assagioli was attracted to developing a scientific discipline and began his training at medical school. As a young man interested in the work of Freud, he was dissatisfied with the limitations of psycho-analysis and was keen to develop a scientific psychology which 'encompassed the whole of man'. This psychology was to include creativity and will, joy and wisdom, as well as the impulses and drives. Above all, he wanted it to be practical   and acces-sible. Because of his background, he felt that this psychology should encompass the soul and that this could be used as a tool for self-development rather than self-analysis.

Assagioli was to develop a close relationship with Alice Bailey, a spiritual leader who wrote a number of esoteric books on humanity's spiritual development. He was deeply affected by the psychosocial problems in the world and the Alice Bailey teachings fully embraced this area. Realizing that both global conditions and individual problems were inexorably compounded together, he was keen to share his knowledge with others and set up various education establishments in his own country and within others.

Roberto shared a love of mountaineering, not unlike other thinkers such as Nietzsche and Ruskin, which was also a compelling metaphor for their preoccupation with developing the latent potential lying within humanity. He used the mountain as a model for our relationship with the superconsciousness in his work and referred to this as 'Psychological Mountain Climbing'.

Assagioli was naturally interested in the Kabbalah, an esoteric and mystical component of the Jewish tradition which his spiritual life was embedded in. Sometimes in his work he would refer to a period of great inner struggling in which all meaning seemed lost, sometimes known as the 'Dark Night of the Soul' or the 'abyss' (see Chapters 11 and 12). In the Kabbalah the 'abyss' precedes the final crossing from duality to Oneness. It is the 'Dweller on the Threshold'. In the abyss a great demon called Choronzon is encountered who is the arch demon of false knowledge. To cross the abyss you need to leave all that you have known behind which is the task facing the initiate on the spiritual path.

As Above, So Below

Assagioli's famous egg diagram was a model of the psyche from a psychosynthesis perspective. Although he only intended it as a 'crude and elementary picture', its permanence and popularity lay within its efficacy in illustrating what could be seen initially as a complex model of consciousness.

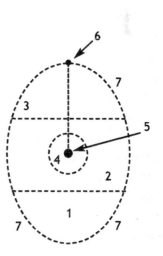

1. *The Lower Unconscious* is made up of subliminal drives, complexes and primitive urges that propel the personality towards achieving certain goals. Within this almost primeval soup lie phobias, obsessions and paranoid delusions and dream content.

2. *The Middle Unconscious* is much more accessible to everyday waking consciousness. This can be likened to liminal space where experiences are assimilated and awaiting to come to light.

3. *The Higher Unconscious* is where we receive our intuition and highest creative and inspirational insights. When we are in touch with this area, our ethical conscience is awakened and there is a strong call to 'service'.

4. *The Field of Consciousness* is where our everyday awareness resides.

5. The Conscious self or 'I' is the centre of our being, a point of pure self awareness and will. It is a reflection of the Self.

6. *The Self* is above and outside the stream of contents passing through everyday consciousness. It is that part of us that is unaffected by the everyday experiences of life. It can be equated to the Spirit.

7. *The Collective Unconscious* is similar to Jung's collective unconscious where one is impacted on by the changing contents of the 'sea' we are immersed in. The membrane that surrounds the egg is porous, allowing for 'psychological osmosis' to take place.

Although the fundamental principle of psychosynthesis is that Self is an ontological being which is both transcendent and immanent, Assagioli warned against the tendency for students and practitioners in becoming too polarized towards self-realization. His background in psychodynamic psychology and the importance of developing a strong enough ego container, had taught him the importance of grounding. He saw that, because of painful historical trauma, there could be a tendency to split off from challenging material in the unconscious and an impulse to veer towards 'mystical flight'. He emphasized the importance of balance in all aspects of psychosynthesis and postulated that it was only in grounding insights and realizations that any true progress could be made.

He saw how the upper and lower aspects of the unconscious were complementary and worked together. Whatever was activated in the upper unconscious through meditation and visualization exercises would have an effect on the lower unconscious which could result in turbulence within the personality as various defense mechanisms holding unconscious material struggled to gain dominion. Always the Self was striving for greater union and harmony. Similarly, work on the level of the personality where the student is striving to harness challenging forces in his make-up, will affect the higher unconscious, bringing insight, strength and joy to the troubled personality.

This underscores the biblical maxim: 'As above, so below' where the kingdom of heaven is not just reflected on the earth, but immanent therein.

Within this next section, *Going Deeper*, I want to embrace the very real spiritual journey that we make as individuals and the changes of consciousness that can be experienced within this context. I use the story of the *Odyssey* to illustrate the trials and tasks that beset us in service of strengthening the soul. As the spiritual path is not an easy one, I highlight some of the problems and insights we may face.

Part III

Chapter 9

Going Deeper

Having spent much of my childhood by the sea and grown accustomed to its moods and cyclical nature, I have come to look upon the sea as a rich metaphor for our spiritual journey in life. There are times when we feel very little is happening in our lives as we go about our daily routine waiting for the tide to come in and take us forward onto the next part of our journey. At these times we may feel abandoned, lonely, our life devoid of meaning and purpose. Other times the tide rushes in, taking us by surprise and we are swept along on a vast wave of change that is exhilarating, even terrifying in places so that we long for some of the peace we might have experienced before. Other times we may have built up a worthwhile occupation for ourselves on the shores in the form of a family or career only to find, almost overnight, a storm has pushed violently in, smashing our carefully honed foundations to pieces and leaving us stranded on an unfamiliar shore.

It is tempting and perhaps human nature to take our way of life for granted and forget about the sea that, although not immediate visible, surrounds us. We may have become unconscious to the wider perspective of life and 'fallen asleep', just as we remember the heroes and heroines doing in our fairy tales. So we are quite unprepared when the tsunami rushes into our neatly charted life and rips open the foundations so that our life as we had known it collapses into the sand. As a result, our life is changed so dynamically, that there is no going back to the old way of life, but only a naked trust in the new untraversed tide that waits to carry us forward. Our fear is that we wonder how we can survive the future without skills and knowledge to support us. The trust and surrender which that necessitates become the raw skills with which we navigate the uncharted waters before us. And like the oyster's pearl, the wisdom which emerges from this time of frustration and inevitable loss, takes the place of the worldly knowledge we thought we had, but which did not serve us in the midst of disaster.

Since this is a book about depression, the reader may wonder what these reflections of the sea have to do with it. As well as being a metaphor for the spiritual journey, the depths, peaks, waves and cyclical nature of the sea, governed by its endless tides provides a rich repository of insight into the nature of depressive illness. In fact, depression has long been known as the 'night sea journey', undertaken very much in the unconscious state, sometimes referred to as the 'Dark Night of the Soul'. Seamus Heaney, the poet, used the term 'Night Ferry' to describe fellow poet, Robert Powell, and wrote:

You were our night ferry
Thudding in a big sea,
The whole craft ringing
With an armourer's music
The course set willfully across
The ungovernable and dangerous.

Sea Journey as Metaphor

The sea journey is a perilous one with multiple trials and tribulations. Although its navigation demands a great deal of courage and determination, very few voyagers feel they possess the degree of inner strength that such a journey warrants. But on a deeper level, each voyage undertaken leads the voyager through what Keats described as 'the vale of soul-making'. And where soul is made, the mundane rules of the world no longer apply. Whether the voyager wants it or not, worldly qualities like bravery and strength are, through the sea initiation, transmuted into soul qualities of wisdom, forbearance, resilience, and insight. This is the nature of soul-making. Soul is intimately connected with the element of water, as like water, the soul takes the shape of the form it pours itself into. I want to include here a quote from White Eagle which cogently describes the making of soul and its mode of expression:

> Once spirit comes down to dwell, it commences the creation of what is called 'soul'. Soul is the creation of feeling. Soul can be described as the feminine aspect of life, the Mother principle existent in human beings, both men and women.

A deeper implication of the sea as a powerful element in the depressive's life is the attraction it has in the thoughts of those who are suicidal, where there is a desperate ongoing yearning to return to the sea. A psychiatrist once discussed this with me when he admitted that the single fantasy that many suicidal patients had, was an overwhelming longing to return to the sea. He equated this with a longing to return to the amniotic sac in the womb. On a deeper level, I see this as a returning to the Great Mother, the source of all life, where the sea's rhythmic process mirrors the ebb and flow of the spiritual journey. We can discern in times of great crises, there is a deep yearning within the soul to return to its source. Although there is nothing wrong with this yearning, in the case of the suicidal person this longing is enacted on the wrong level, on the level of personality rather than the level of Self.

Kay Redfield Jamison, in her work about suicide, refers to an 'Odysseus agreement' which can be drawn up in some areas of the United States. This is a contract which the patient sets in motion in the form of a written agreement when they are of rational mind to come into effect when they have a depressive episode and are suicidal. This may include mandatory treatment in the form of antipsychotic medications, or electroconvulsive therapy which they are unlikely to consent to when they are of unsound mind. She writes 'This is based on the mythic character's request to be strapped to the mast of the ship so that he might avoid the inevitable call of the Sirens'. Odysseus agreements (or advanced instruction directives) allow patients to agree to certain treatments in advance.

In the myth, Odysseus could have plugged his ears with wax to resist the calls, but he chose to be bound to the ship's mast instead. This is because he thought the song of the Sirens was so beautiful that, despite the dangers, he still wanted to hear the song. In the context of this chapter, Odysseus still wanted to hear the song of his 'spiritual homeland' even though he knew it would make him want to sever the ties with the earthly world with all its trials and tribulations.

The Odyssey

As myth and psychology create the interface for depth psychology, I want to use the story of Odysseus as a metaphor for our relationship with our spiritual journey, or odyssey. Here, Ithaca, is our spiritual home that we are contracted to return to.

Odysseus, the warrior king, after a ten year battle in Troy, was preparing to make the journey home to Ithaca with his crew to be re-united with his wife Penelope and Telemachus, his son. As Homer relates, Odysseus, the hero of the story, was clever and skilful with a thirst for adventure and the fame that winning conquests bestowed on him.

Not long into his quest, Odysseus landed at a Thracian port, Ismarus slew its people and took possession of its wives and valuables. This wanton act of greed and savagery evoked the wrath of the father of the Gods, Zeus. Deciding that Odysseus wasn't ready to return home, Zeus beset him with various trials which were a nemesis for what he had done. Great winds were unleashed so that Odysseus and his crew were washed up on a shore of an idyllic island which quickly worked its charm on his crew. If it had not been for Mercury's intervention, warning him against eating the lotus flowers that, once ingested, wove a spell of forgetfulness over the eater, he would have succumbed and never returned home. He would have forgotten who he was and where he was going.

After landing on the island of the Cyclopes, inhabited by a race of one eyed giants, and slaying the leader who threatened to eat his men, then visiting the underworld and many other adventures, Odysseus was weary and longed to return home. But just as he was within a couple of days of reaching the Turkish port, once again strong winds swept him hundreds of miles off course and his fleet of ships together with his crew were wrecked and lost. This was a curse bestowed upon him by the relentless and unforgiving Poseidon, god of the seas and earthquakes. Odysseus didn't know that the Cyclopes he slew was, in fact, Poseidon's son, Polyphemus. Poseidon was infuriated by this act, especially by the way in which Odysseus had boasted of his conquest afterwards. The loss of his crew and ship were further nemesis from the Gods again.

Wearily, Odysseus, the only survivor, is washed up on an island called Scheria. There, he is nursed back to health by a beautiful nymph, Calypso. Despite his intentions to return home, Odysseus finds himself seduced by the beautiful Calypso and the paradisiacal life of the island.

When, after seven years, Odysseus begins longing for his wife, child and his home again, Calypso offers him the greatest temptation she can offer: a mortal-eternal life where he can live as one of the Gods and never grow old.

But Odysseus is resolute and Calypso reluctantly provides him with the materials to return home. By then nearly twenty years have passed and what was going to be a two week journey to return from Troy to Ithaca had taken eight years. But when Odysseus does return home to his wife and son, he has changed. All the pride and arrogance over his conquest of Troy has turned to ashes and means nothing to him. Within their place has grown humility and deep longing for something that the world, with all its glory and adventure, could not give him. He is in actuality experiencing a 'divine homesickness' which can present itself as depression or deep sadness that underpins all the realized and unrealized ambitions and goals of the world.

Since all these characters are intrapsychic, we can examine them more closely. Odysseus, like all of us, has a calling in life to undertake some task in service of the planetary evolution and ultimately in service of the Self. But he became so identified with the prestige that the world offered him that he began to value this above his spiritual home and here the dialogue between the Self became jeopardized as he identified more with the wants and desires of the personality. He suffered nemesis after his fatal landing at the Thracian port. But even within the context of this redemptive journey, Odysseus was in dialogue with the Self in the form of Mercury who intervened to warn him of the Lotus Eaters. These were a fabulous people living in Africa who had eaten lotus flowers which rendered them forgetful of their life journey and reduced them to a state of happy indolence. In the story several of Odysseus' men had eaten them and were dragged weeping back to their ship after they had forgotten who they were and where they were going. If he had eaten them, he would have forgotten who he was, a spiritual being experiencing the earth, and never woken to full consciousness or returned home.

In the context of this book it can be seen that Odysseus was suffering both a *spiritual emergency* and a *spiritual emergence* (see Chapter 10).

The spiritual emergency presents itself in the form of the very real psychic experiences he was engaged with. And it was through this violent passage of longing and suffering that a spiritual emergence was taking place. This emergence was in the longing to return home and although it had never really gone away, it had been eclipsed by unconsciousness as he became more identified with his personality. Towards the end of the story, Odysseus resists the ultimate temptation of being a God which, enacted on the personality level, would cause him to be too grandiose and arrogant to make that journey home. He had, through suffering and loss, learned humility which 'brings with it an attitude of reverence which enables us to surrender our personal will'. Through humility the connection with the Self emerges and there is a surrendering to Divine Will. Humility is an integral part of the spiritual path. Without it, like Odysseus, we fall into spiritual pride. This longing or 'divine homesickness' is experienced in the heart and as the personality surrenders to the Self the moral imperative is activated. Within this context the meaning of the journey or Odyssey is understood. The trials and tribulations are seen as proving ground to move from the status of 'hero' to that of a 'guide' who can facilitate the spiritual emergence of others. In the next chapter we will look at the concept of spiritual emergency and emergence.

Chapter 10

Spiritual Emergency to Spiritual Emergence

The reason I have included spiritual emergency and emergence here is that depressive illness can both precipitate a spiritual emergence and also be one of the factors which triggers off a spiritual emergency. Depression is closely entwined with spirituality since both are precipitated by altered states of consciousness. These states of internal crisis were terms created by psychiatrist Stanislav Grof in the 1980s. Grof worked a lot with psychiatric patients who were depressed, or undergoing trauma linked with earlier childbirth (perinatal) experiences or incidents which had brought them up against the edge of death. He believed that spiritual emergence and emergency were part of a natural process, often determined by perinatal and near death experiences. His insight into these realms of non-ordinary states of consciousness created inroads and maps for the understanding of psychosis, schizophrenia and depressive conditions.

Spiritual practice is by no means an easy or straightforward path. It is a way of life that demands dedication, discrimination and where the meeting with disillusionment isn't uncommon. Here I am reminded of how moths are attracted to bright lights, mistaking them for the light of the moon with which they use to navigate. The moths, dazzled by the false light, become dizzy and confused and batter their fragile wings and even impale themselves on the light in an effort to attain its brilliance.

Although the spiritual path may offer us a respite from the struggle of the material world, it is not a permanent resting place or an escape from our troubles. Like any new relationship we embark on in life there is a 'honeymoon' period which, in concrete terms, lasts about a year, but then the work sets in. I remember a friend of mine who joined AA saying that she had been told that the first year is 'free', but after that you need to start putting in the work in order to progress. After the honeymoon period there is a drop-off rate as people get disillusioned with the path they are following. It is as if the light that first attracted us to the journey is actually beginning to highlight the areas within our personality and life that need to be transformed in order to benefit from the path. Work on the self can be too daunting and the honeymooners leave to follow another path or direction. This path-hopping can prolong the inner work that needs to be done for an indefinite period. But each time the honeymoon period becomes shorter and as disillusionment sets in, the path-hopper faces crises of meaning where he cannot go any further until he confronts everything he has run away from. Even then, some people will resist this process and either abandon the whole idea of spiritual practice, which is hard since something has been wakened, or return to fulfill a more meaningful career in the world. Still others, who often have a great sensitivity to the energies of the superconscious but lack the discipline and resolution to develop this further, escape into drugs and alcohol which, initially, may provide some sort of temporary relief before the shadow side of addiction kicks in.

But when does a recreational drug become addictive?

It is worth remembering that underpinning the drug culture is a call of the Self, to deeper meaning. The error is interpreting the call on the level of the personality rather than the Self.

Writer and Buddhist, Jack Kornfield, cites a story about Chogyam Trungpa Rinpoche who, at the start of a talk he was giving in Berkley, asked the large hall of people how many had just begun spiritual practice. To the raised hands he said, "My suggestion is that you go home! At the back door, they will give you your money back and you can go home and not get started in this very difficult and terrible process."

This spiritual teacher went on to warn of the difficulties that confronted a disciple on the path. But once the journey has begun, the call to Self has been heard, it is equally hard not to pursue the path because all the bright baubles of the mundane world have lost their attraction and one's eyes have been opened to another journey, another horizon.

I have rarely found that the dangers of the spiritual path are ever highlighted. In every other walk of life potential risks are recognized and warnings issued. Taking out insurance cover for accidents, thefts, injuries from anything in the home, to holiday and work situations is mandatory and so much a part of our lifestyle that we don't give this a second thought. Yet when it comes to protecting oneself against spiritual emergency, soul loss and disappointment, we laugh at the idea. Perhaps this is one of the problems endemic in a modern spirituality that has left the cloisters for the marketplace where one can only take responsibility for oneself, rather than being held responsible for anyone else. We can implement insurance policies in cyberspace, but we haven't found a way of insuring the safety of the soul. I think that the resistance to pointing out the dangers in opening up to spiritual practice says a lot about our Western obsession and preoccupation with the light and the exile of the shadow.

We forget that in the centre of the guiding flame is the shadow, a compelling metaphor for the world of duality. Until we accept the shadow within ourselves we cannot but react in an ignorance-based fear when we see it in the world.

In Marian Caplan's book, *Halfway up the Mountain*, with the compelling subtitle, *The Error of Premature Claims to Enlightenment*, Andrew Cohen writes about our own private fantasy of enlightenment that can get in the way of inner development. Here, he makes a clear distinction between 'personal' and 'impersonal enlightenment'. In personal enlightenment there is a drive for personal gain. The enlightenment is desired because 'I' want to be the 'one', the one that knows. The second impersonal enlightenment is reached through a pure heart where the personality surrenders to the Self and the intention is to be of service for the sake of all beings. Forcing and hurrying organic processes in nature have a detrimental effect on the environment as we know, how much more this must affect the soul when it is forced to emerge too quickly; energies are unleashed that are out of control; Spirit is numinous, bright and fiery and is regarded as sacred for good reason. Our ancestors invoked the help of the spiritual realms through wise priests and shamans. Spirituality can be tempered in the form of a candle flame, but unleashed it can burn like a forest fire, ruthlessly consuming its maker.

I am always touched by the respect with which firemen talk about fire when they give their mandatory fire lectures at the hospital where I work. They know all about protection and safety measures because their lives and the lives of others depend on it. Whenever I come out of a fire lecture I am reminded that fire is a living presence and needs to be properly harnessed. I cannot help but use this as a metaphor for the spiritual path; tread carefully and diligently. This reminds me of the kundulini energy which lies coiled at the base of the spine. White Eagle says:

The meaning of the word, Kundulini, is 'ball of fire'. This ball of fire lies in the body of every human being, sleeping undis-turbed until the individual commences to develop spiritually.

Daily meditation is a tried and tested technique of developing one's spiritual practice. Here, there is a steady chipping away at the rough ashlar of the personality which masks the 'imprisoned splendor'. But sometimes, through various powerful meditative and yogic techniques, a rupturing of the thin veil between the inner world and outer world takes place, flinging the unprepared individual into a state of spiritual emergency. This can also happen spontaneously through a trauma or major change in one's personal life, such as bereavement, childbirth, career change or through the volatile energies awakened in adolescence. Alternatively, a spiritual emergency may come as a result of a breakdown on a physical or mental level. Without warning, a person finds themselves in a terrifying world where there are no boundaries between what is taking place internally and what is happening outwardly. There is a psychic opening through which the hapless individual may find clairaudient and clairvoyant impressions flooding through. Unable to process the volume of internal material, they may find themselves in a transitory state of psychosis where inner and outer reality becomes conflated. These spiritual emergencies can become frightening and intolerable by the fear and lack of understanding of well-meaning relatives and friends. Exacerbating this even more is the obsessional need to heal and fix the condition from healthcare professionals who perceive the whole process as a sickness rather than dis-ease in the soul. It seems that the person suffering spiritual emergency has to deal with everyone else's state of neurotic emergency too!

Sadly, people who can facilitate and guide the person who is undergoing spiritual emergency are few and far between. Even a psychotherapist, who does not include the transpersonal aspect to their practice, will look upon a spiritual emergency as a breakthrough of some long suppressed biographical trauma or abuse. I have known people who have spent years working through 'childhood abuse' in therapy that didn't actually exist in order to cure the spiritual emergency. I have known still others who have had their visions and psychic expression suppressed by powerful medication.

It seems ironical that our ancestors used drugs to initiate some powerful rite of passage into adulthood and now our modern age uses drugs to suppress these very same symptoms. Is it any wonder that the drug taking culture amongst our young has increased in the absence of rites of passage which were a way of guiding the young into the terrain of adulthood? The shamans, the wise men and women that guided the young through the critical thresholds of sexual, emotional and psychic development, have long been disempowered by a culture that desacralises the world.

Fortunately, there are and have been therapists and psychiatrists that recognize the distinctions between genuine pathological illness and spiritual opening and, furthermore, allow this psychospiritual perspective to guide their practice. I want to look at the work of these pioneers in psychospiritual development in the light of spiritual emergency and emergence.

Stanislav Grof: A Psychiatrist with Insight

In the 1980s non-ordinary states of consciousness where there was psychic opening and individuals were having psychotic episodes as a result of this, were regarded by professionals in the mental health field as mentally ill. Psychiatrists studied their patients' inner experience through the lens of pathological illness and were unable to see that what was happening to the patient was part of a much broader dynamic. As a result, many individuals, who were experiencing altered states of consciousness (ASC), were afraid of being labeled as mentally unstable and avoided medical intervention, preferring to tough out their experience on their own where possible. Without any real external support or understanding of what was going on, these experiences were more debilitating, driving some to become suicidal and others to deeper feelings of paranoia and isolation.

Stanislav Grof had spent thirty years working with patients having these non-ordinary states of consciousness. In the 1950s Grof became part of the leading edge research project in Prague into the therapeutic effects of LSD on psychiatric patients. After self experimenting with LSD he discovered that much of the psychic material he was experiencing was identical to the experiential material he had read about in shamanic and tribal rituals. Furthermore, a lot of what he was experiencing through LSD was identical to the content described by schizophrenics. There was a remarkable correlation between the experiences of people with psychosis, shamanic ritual and LSD-induced experiences. These controlled experiments with the patient's consent, allowed him to see beyond the *biographical story* which might have elicited such altered states of unreality in the patient, and dip into the *spiritual journey* of each individual. He encountered past life memories that were stored in the unconscious and perinatal experiences. These often traumatic perinatal memories of birth tapped into a deeper process of life and death. He found that if the patient was supported in his non-ordinary state of consciousness, rather than having it suppressed through medication, a miraculous healing took place. Previously, hospitalized patients who were resistant to conventional methods of treatment not only recovered from their states of unreality but actually became stronger through it all. In some instances, they were able to go on and help others engaging in similar experiences.

Grof concluded that if a patient received the support and understanding they needed within their spiritual emergency, this would be sufficient to carry them through the threshold of spiritual emergence. A remarkable transformation was taking place within the individual consciousness. In conventional psychiatric terms, the patient had emerged from a psychotic state and had returned to normality. Through his own experience Grof believed that these states of being were not only an integral but a natural process happening within the individual psyche. Rather than being a mental illness, 'it may actually be the organism's radical effort to right itself'. He concluded that in many cases it wasn't that the patient had a problem, but in our culture we have an inability to accept anything or anyone outside our insular perspective of reality: a reality that relegates what may be a normal state of being to a place devoid of acceptance and understanding. No wonder altered states of consciousness have become so feared and carry such a burden of shame.

In many ways, the rites of passage, performed within our ancient civilizations, marked critical thresholds to higher orders of reality. People, namely shamans, wise people, healers and priests who could voluntarily access these realms of altered consciousness, were respected and listened to.

Where have these same people gone in the twentieth century?

They have either gone into hiding or have been fortunate, like Stan Grof, to find a niche for their abilities by working as a healer or therapist. But more often than not, we look at these same people through the lens of suppressive medication and psychiatric labeling in an effort to exile ourselves further from a reality that is too frightening to allow in.

It was through his witnessing various states of spirituality that he decided to create an interface between this and his scientific background. He referred to this as transpersonal psychology (see Chapter 7).

Mythology as an Interface

It was the late mythologist, Joseph Campbell, who first introduced Stanislav Grof to Christina who was to become his future wife. She was also to become a key figure in moving his work closer to spiritual emergency. Joseph Campbell had been contacted by Christina, a former student of his, who was in desperate need to make sense of the grueling inner experiences she had undergone for several years. Campbell knew that Christina wasn't suffering from psychosis because she was able to observe what was taking place within her rationally. She realised that the experiences, terrifying though they were, were not being instigated from an outside agency but they were taking place within her. This is the major discriminating feature of those suffering from full-blown psychosis, where the agents of their internal experiences are perceived as coming from outside, hence the feelings of paranoid delusion. What Campbell did know was that many of the experiences she was undergoing were identical to the ones experienced within the initiation thresholds into tribal practice. He knew this because of his research into tribal practices and mythologies, but also because he was in touch with another eminent psychiatrist called John Weir Perry.

Perry, who had lived in different cultures himself, namely China and Africa, had a deep understanding of tribal initiations, where the initiate would go through a series of outer difficulties, in the form of tortuous rituals and exile from his family tribe. Although these practices were brutal, they were also necessary in breaking down the ego structure of the individual so that he or she could experience a different internal reality. Normally, all our cultural injunctions protect us from our internal world by developing an ego that only identifies with *activity* and *doing*, rather than *being*, as in meditation and yogic practices; the initiates would experience a schizophrenic breakdown where they lost touch with the identity that they had known before the experience. This was often mirrored by a formal severance of contact with their historical family members.

Pathological and Tribal Schizophrenia
Divested of his past and his identity, the initiate was ready to enter another reality – the reality of the tribe. Campbell wanted to know what it was that held the difference between the pathological schizophrenia of today and the schizophrenia of the initiate in the tribe or the shaman. He decided that the difference was that the shaman or tribal initiate learned to swim in what Jung named the 'collective archetypal' sea, whereas the schizophrenic, trapped in a culture that saw what he was experiencing as sickness, drowned. Christina, despite the grueling conditions

she found herself in the midst of, was swimming! She was able to hold on to her outer reality by bringing up two children and to know enough about the psychiatric field to shun it in preference to a spiritual approach.

Spiritual Emergency Triggered by Childbirth
Christina's experiences had begun when she had birthed her first child, four years previously. And certainly childbirth experiences can trigger off powerful psychic forces trapped within the soul memory. Post partum depression is dangerously debilitating and can be a prelude to a spiritual emergency. In the midst of giving birth to her son, she was suddenly gripped by a powerful and overwhelming energy that had her shaking from head to toe. Her breathing changed, her body seemed to move of its own accord and brilliant lights and visions exploded into her brain. Within this state she experienced a mixture of bliss and terror: bliss from the powerful energy she found herself in the midst of and terror that she was going mad. This experience repeated two years later when she had her second child and five years after that when she had a car accident and she was brought up against the interface of life and death and faced her own mortality.

Unable to continue living a normal life or return to the person she was before the experiences, she underwent major life changes of divorcing her husband and beginning a new life on her own where she felt even more isolated and estranged from reality. Just as her inner experiences could be beautiful, they were also excruciatingly painful and at times her body seemed racked with pain. Throughout, she was having visions and experiencing changes in consciousness, yet working its way through all this internal chaos was the very real fear she would end up in a mental institution.

Meeting Grof was a great relief for her as his work with altered states of consciousness in psychiatric patients seemed to normalize and make sense of her experience. Grof believed she was undergoing a spiritual emergency and the worst thing she could do was suppress the material. With patience, he helped her to work with the material, rather than against it. This process was to last Christina all of fourteen years which was a large part of her life. At this time she also realized that much of the physical phenomena she was experiencing along with the visions were an awakening of her kundulini, which seemed to have become triggered off during that first childbirth. In fact, as Christina's work moved more into the field of spiritual emergency, she found that her experiences were to become her work.

I have to say here that although there are many cases of spiritual emergency, not all of them are as violent or as lengthy as Christina's. Rather than being a condition that had been brought on by spiritual practice of any sort, it happened involuntarily and yet the fact that it became an integral part of her journey, work and teaching, suggests that this manifested a special training ground for her, painful though it may seem. The people who facilitate in any therapeutic enterprise rarely choose such a training ground voluntarily, although, according to some schools of esoteric thought, the soul will have done so before entering incarnation. Rather, the training ground and the life work that it brings chooses them!

A Psychotic Episode or Spiritual Emergency

In proportion as prophecy is higher and more perfect than divination... in the same proportion.... Is madness superior to the sane mind, for the one is only of human, but the other of divine origin.
Plato

I would like to illustrate a distinction between a psychotic episode and a state of spiritual emergency.

Grof described the difference between someone undergoing spiritual emergency rather than a psychotic episode as 'the ability to differentiate to a *considerable* degree between inner experiences and the world of consensus reality'. In this, they are able to attribute the courses of their changed reality to inner experiences, rather than external ones. The psychotic is unable to do this and projects his/her disturbing experience onto something outside in the form of paranoia and persecution. Even so, non-psychotics can experience 'transitory psychosis', John Weir Perry, Californian psychiatrist, believed. He expanded on Jung's premise that psychosis was a temporary state of dis-ease which was an effort of the psyche to right itself. Like Grof, he had found, in his work with young people undergoing psychotic episodes, that, when given the compassion and understanding they needed, they emerged, soon after, completely well. He firmly believed that psychosis was an inner journey which was once accepted in tribal practices, but banned from our rigid societal paradigm today. He expresses this cogently in his book, *The Far Side of Madness*:

If psychiatry could learn to cooperate with rather than combat nature, we might be of more benefit to persons meeting their developmental crises... Then, too, the psyche can get on with its work without having to combat an uncomprehending environment.

The single most exciting point here was that Perry held the psychotic episode in a spiritual context. He further illustrates:

When the soul is born into the world it is inclined to forget it's previously acquired vision of the divine light of heaven and must enter into these extraordinary mad states in order to retrieve what it has lost.

However, it takes an experienced 'guide' who is aware of the interface between psychosis and spiritual emergency to make that distinction. Assagioli delineates another clear distinction between pathological disturbance and 'transitory psychosis' by suggesting that the recipient's experiences are mainly 'regressive' in nature, in that after the incident he/she will remain unchanged and go back to his/her old patterns of behavior and thinking. In spiritual emergency these are likely to be 'progressive' in that there is awakening in consciousness in the form of self-realization which is life changing.

Stanislav Grof and John Perry's exploration of these altered states coincided with a monumental explosion of drug-induced experiences in the 1960s which, in a sense, normalized psychotic episodes; psychedelic 'tripping' legitimized the validity of a psychotic episode. However, taking unsupervised drugs without any understanding of what is happening is a dangerous and foolhardy affair. Although some experimenters were able to safely negotiate the stormy waters between the content of their outer and inner worlds, many of a more sensitive disposition were less likely to do this. This ability to navigate between levels of being and consciousness had a lot to do with the strength of one's ego container. Where there was fragmentation through historical schisms in the parenting structure, particularly with mothers who cut off from their feelings and emotions, there was a tendency to be overwhelmed by the experience and drown in the content. Doors that had been locked in the psyche were flung open and the fragmented ego descended into chaos that, without proper guidance, necessitated psychiatric intervention. Like any intense experience, drug-induced changes in consciousness leave their markers on the psyche, the doors once opened never entirely shut again.

Perhaps our ancestors understood the necessity of maintaining barriers and respected the strength of the inner world which, in the old psychiatric paradigm, is still classified as madness. And here Perry talks about a secondary madness that has denigrated the inner world 'as a bland impoverishment and narrowness, in which the conventions and concreteness of the mundane world are taken for self evident reality'.

In order to make an informed diagnosis in the case of depressive psychoses (bipolar disorder), various medical conditions such as diabetes mellitus, thyroid disorder, dementia and pernicious anemia need to be professionally eliminated. This is because these illnesses can produce similar symptoms as those in spiritual emergency.

Spiritual Emergency and the Dark Night of the Soul

Before moving onto Roberto Assagioli's work on spiritual awakening, I want to discuss another distinction between spiritual emergency and the 'Dark Night of the Soul'. From my research into the 'Dark Night of the Soul', this is a more gradual progressive event, whereas a spiritual emergency is, as its name implies a crisis, affecting body, mind and spirit. This crisis is largely psychic in texture and invasive. In the 'Dark Night of the Soul' experience the recipient is looking for spiritual contact, is hungering for it and this is more often a conscious knowledge. In spiritual emergency, the circumstances the subject finds themselves in can be violent, catatonic and forceful. The recipient may be totally unaware of any need for spiritual contact, even avoiding it. Although they might be interested in developing psychic powers, psychism is very different to spirituality.

Although Assagioli had been toiling away in the background for many years, perhaps it was significant that his work became more widely known during the 1960s when there was a burgeoning interest in the spiritual path. This was when recreational drugs like cannabis were used to facilitate the transcendent mood as demonstrated by the iconic Beatles. Assagioli took spiritual awakening seriously and divided the process into four critical and distinct stages:

- Crisis preceding spiritual awakening

- Crises caused by the spiritual awakening
- Reactions following the spiritual awakening
- Dark Night of the Soul

Crisis Preceding Spiritual Awakening

A crisis within the personality and soul can occur through a steady progressive sense of disillusionment with life. This can happen in the midst of material success and relative wealth where the individual can wonder what life is all about. Having reached a plateau in their material life where they *should* be happy, the individual experiences a sense of 'something missing'. One is faced with the archetypal questions: 'What does this all serve?' 'What is this life for?' As time goes by, there is a deepening sense of emptiness which no amount of distractive forays in the everyday world can dislodge. As hard as one tries to ignore the rising sense of nihilism in one's life, the subject finds themselves called, time and time again, back to finding meaning and purpose in life. It is a hunger that, once wakened, can give them no respite. Often, through a long and painful process of soul searching, the individual begins to develop an interest in spiritual affairs and may go in search of a teacher. Where this stage used to be part of a mid-life crises occurring in the late thirties, early forties, it is now being reached earlier by men and women in their twenties.

Crisis Caused by the Spiritual Awakening

The cornerstone to successfully integrating this material exists in the ability to hold the experience in proper perspective. Say, for example, someone has attended their first ever spiritual retreat and the experience has been so powerful that the individual is unable to process it adequately. The ego, which may have been fragmented during abuse, trauma and loss within the childhood environment, is not fully able to contain the energies evoked. Consequently, the subject falls under the spell of the mistaken belief that they have been 'chosen' to fulfill some deeply spiritual mission in life. They may even believe that they are special with messianic qualities. St John of the Cross urges the importance of not becoming too taken in by the psychic content of spiritual awakening. It is perhaps sufficient to say that where there has been a peak in consciousness, there is also the complimentary 'fall' waiting in the wings. Falls are needed to earth material and insights. Grounding is absolutely key to the integration of these experiences.

Reactions to the Spiritual Awakening
These vary according to the individual and force of the awakening. Besides a new found sense of rightness and peace with the life, there is a sense of deep joy. But gradually, as time goes by, these feelings ebb as all experiences are organic and cyclical in nature. Assagioli writes:

> Because of the synthesizing nature, the superconscious energies act on the personality in ways that tend to bring them to their next higher level of organization. When this higher level is reached, synergic energy is released and this energy in turn produces the ecstasy, elation, and joy characteristic of such experiences.

In some cases, if the spiritual awakening has been powerful enough and the personality able to sustain the inflow of impressions, there may be a complete transformation in the person that is lasting in nature. Here, Assagioli cites that permanent changes are rare. In most cases, after the energy has subsided, the individual reverts back to his/her old ways, although he/she now has a blueprint to follow. At the least, the spiritual awakening may be enough to discern what is 'missing' in the life. Here, the individual is 'called' to realize deeper meaning in life.

As sunlight always reveals the dust motes and the smears on

the window pane, so does the spiritual awakening reveal flaws in the personality which are blocking its way to further growth. The temptation here is to become hypercritical of ones own defects and the defects of others, neither of which bring one any peace of mind, rather than seeing this as an opportunity to augment necessary changes in ones life. Too much is ventured too quickly, rather like crash dieting where weight loss is neither permanent nor healthy. The other temptation is a 'repression of the sublime', which is to deny that anything has happened. And here Assagioli urges that this disillusionment is a natural part of the process.

Assagioli stresses the importance of the individual having a spiritual guide or mentor who knows the journey and can steer them through the wilderness of self-condemnation or through feelings of being 'special' or 'chosen'. A guiding friend or therapist can bring them into safe harbor so that they can integrate their experiences. The guide's role is to enable the client to balance the regressive and progressive energies within themselves that the experience may have evoked. The regressive experience may present itself in self-obsessed thoughts and an introverted withdrawal from daily life which may be all right for a while, but when carried to excess, exacerbate feelings of alienation and being different. The guide's task is to enable the client to make sense of the experience and work with the material through visualization exercises and most of all, begin to ground it in everyday practice. Grounding can present itself through the model of service which also guards against the tendency to self-analyses and makes it possible to create simple goals in the 'here' and 'now' by keeping a journal or joining a self help group.

I want to include here two case histories which serve to illustrate spiritual emergency followed by spiritual emergence.

Rita was 25 years old and had suffered prolonged bouts of suicidal depression since she was seventeen. She was an intelligent, creative young woman who had just moved from

Scotland to North Yorkshire with her husband's job. At the time, her husband was working down in Birmingham for six weeks, returning every weekend. Rita, having just moved to the area, had no family or friends nearby and found herself very isolated. She visited her GP because of insomnia and anxiety. He had recommended that she go along to a local group that were practicing Transcendental Meditation (TM) as he felt this would help her a lot more than medication. This she did and was given a mantra to repeat twice a day. By the second day Rita's depression had gone and been totally eclipsed by an unexplained euphoria in which she felt an overwhelming sense of union with all life. She didn't sleep that night because she had brilliant light flashing through her head and she was experiencing Christ-like visions. Ringing up the TM centre and asking if this was usual, they assured her that this did sometimes happen in a very sensitive individual and to cut the mantra down from fifteen minutes twice a day to five minutes.

This she did, but the next morning plunged into a suicidal depression that was terrifying and worse than anything she had experienced before as she was aware of dark malevolent forces around her. She lay awake all night, her heart racing for hours on end and her body crippled with agonizing pain as if she was being crucified. After a few hours, she could feel this subsiding and being replaced by a deep peace and sense of wellbeing. Gradually, this deepened into a state of euphoria. Apart from somebody visiting from the nearest TM centre, some twenty miles away, and asking if she had tried taking Rescue Remedy, there was no help available. Finding that she had lost the strength in her legs, she found herself crawling to the phone and ringing for a doctor to come out and prescribe something for her. Unable to articulate what was going on for her, he suggested she started looking for a job.

In a week she lost a stone.

In two weeks she had lost nearly two stone and looked as if she had stepped out of a prisoner of war camp... The only thing that kept her going was her dog, Rex, who needed feeding and was a support to her. If she couldn't get up for herself she would get up for him. Out of desperation, she contacted a spiritual centre for healing and arranged to travel the next day to see them. That night she slept for the first time in weeks and was awoken by a Christ-like vision. The Christ figure touched her and she experienced a spontaneous healing. The healer at the centre admitted that this wasn't the first time she had come across someone in such an 'open' condition. She was told that she was psychically too open and used a special healing technique to close her psychic centers/chakras. Rita became well, the depression lifted and she went regularly to a weekly meditation group that was like a port in the storm after her terrifying ordeal.

This cogently reveals the dangers inherent in the spiritual path. And, although the GP recommended an alternative to medication, it was not the right alternative because she was plunged from despair into a state of spiritual emergency. Fortunately, she was brought to safety through a spiritual network that was aware of the psychic problems due to premature awakening.

This second case history is interesting in that it involves a spiritual awakening that sent Karin into a state of spiritual emergency from which she later emerged.

Karin was a twenty two year old Swedish student at teacher training college. She shared a house with several other students and became friends with the girl in the opposite room. Her name was Anna and she was a girl with strong Christian beliefs. Karin had found from an early age that she had a resistance to the Christian belief, mainly because of all the bloodshed and violence exercised in the name of Christianity. Anna had been insistent in wanting to involve Karin in her spiritual life and Karin had desisted. In a fit of arrogance, she had waved her arm in the air and said, "Okay, if you can prove that the Christ presence is real, I might think again." As she made that statement, she found herself staring directly at a picture of Christ in the room which, simultaneously, seemed to send out a lightening jolt in her body which left her reeling.

In that moment, all her strength seemed to have drained from her so that even holding a glass of water was an effort. This psychic shock opened her senses to things that had been hidden to her before. She experienced an entire drama unfolding within her in which there were visions, filled with both positive and negative energy. She sensed things about people that were confirmed later or came true. Along with that, she was aware of what she could only describe as a fire moving up and down her spine which, with effort, she managed to suppress so that it never rose above her navel. Throughout this she was absolutely terrified. Karin, a self-confessed skeptic before, was to have her mindsets around religion and the spiritual life drastically changed. Having lost a lot of weight and wanting to get rid of the psychic experiences she was having, she went to a spiritual group that friends had recommended to her and experienced a healing that eased the high levels of anxiety.

But despite the healing, she felt she could never go back to how she was before. Instead, she sensed the importance of maintaining a spiritual practice which she had spent so long avoiding. This practice was to become the cornerstone of her life when she finally became a meditation teacher and healer and a greatly valued one as no one knew more than herself about the dangers of premature awakening.

Distinctions between the Self and the Superconscious

Many of the esoteric or inner teachings of the world religions were not entered into until the initiate was mature in years. This was true in the Kabbalah where the pupil had to be at least forty years of age or have had a family or held down a job for some years. All these conferred a maturity and psychological strength. This is the same for psychosynthesis where the ego container needs to be strong enough for the 'I' to emerge and awaken to the energies of the Self; the pupil needed to be tested in the kiln of life experience in order to have the inner strength to withstand the energies that can be evoked from the superconscious.

Superconscious experiences, where people may experience psychic phenomena such as visions or astral projection, do not necessarily confer wisdom unless the material can be integrated on a deeper level. Afterwards, the person may revert back to being exactly the same person as he/she was before the experience. Assagioli theorizes that where the superconscious *descends* into the personal conscious, there may be expansion of consciousness, even genius, but because there is no real self-awareness this will be transitory. In contrast, when the 'I' has, through sustained effort, *ascended* to a superconscious level there is a degree of self-realization. A direct experience of the Self is pure and without content, whereas contact with the superconscious energies may be crowded with content as in psychic experiences.

Distinctions between Mystical Experience and Schizophrenia

Evelyn Underhill defines mysticism as 'the art of union with Reality. The mystic is a person who has attained that union in greater or lesser degree.' She claims that to really know a thing, you need to achieve union with it. The mystical experience is a blissful state that the initiate aspires to through prolonged periods of meditation, sublimation of lower energies and sustained spiritual practice. Usually, the mystic is in conscious control and prepares for the experience by diligent practice. Author of *A Course in Miracles* and clinical psychologist, Underhill defines the distinction between mysticism and schizophrenia by saying that although schizophrenics may be able to re-integrate into society after their experience, they will lack the capacity to understand the 'lesson' of the experience. William James expands on this by saying that 'the expansion of self, which is really loss of self, may be difficult to contend with if the recipient lacks a strong sense of self himself'. Assagioli is clear in pointing out that 'although the mystical experience may arouse the necessary impetus in order to be a carrier of God's work in the world as in the Christian mystics, it is not an end in itself and is a partial experience of the spiritual life'.

Certainly not all mystical experiences are held within an ambience of bliss, light and union; quite the opposite was experienced by St John of the Cross, a mature mystic. His experience of what he referred to as 'Dark Night of the Soul' was severe and relentless and enough to drive anyone over the edge (see Chapter 11). Here, he experienced the most profound trial feared by those on the spiritual path: that of alienation and separation from the Divine.

T.S. Eliot more than hints at this experience in *Four Quartets*: 'I said to my soul, be still and let the dark come upon you/Which shall be the darkness of God.'

Spiritual and Global Emergency Today

I do believe 'spiritual emergency' is increasing and Grof, along with ecopsychologists, ecologists and spiritual leaders, concedes that this is in response to the global crises we have evoked by our exploitation of the environment and third world countries. James Lovelock, in his latest work, *The Revenge of Gaia*, written in the midst of the New Orleans disaster, talks about the critical thresholds we have reached where global change is not only inevitable, but is beginning to take place. Now climatologists believe that we have almost reached the point where adverse and irretrievable changes take place; we can discern this in the spiel of media publications available that concentrate on the melting of ice floes in Greenland and Antarctica. The earth is heating up and we are all part of this dynamic. When heat is applied to anything the molecules become agitated and excited which can be extremely uncomfortable. This, as Lovelock explains, isn't just down to our heedlessness in not taking global warming seriously as the sun rays are becoming more intense. Scientists confirm that in the last sixty years, the sun is brighter than it has ever been, although no one quite knows why. Exacerbating this global problem is the release of millions of tons of carbon dioxide from fossil fuels such as coal and oil. It is as if we are steadily cooking anyway, but only speeding up the process by burying our heads in the sand and hoping the problem will go away. The melting of the ice floes that protect the earth from over heating is jeopardizing our continuity as a race. Globally and climatically we are experiencing an emergency, and if we use the sun's increase in intensity and brightness as a metaphor for the Self shining more brightly to enable us to navigate another critical threshold in planetary consciousness we are, as a race, in a state of spiritual emergency. Society is reacting to this intensifying in an ever growing plethora of symptoms, such as depression, dementia and psychosis, as characterized in our young and elderly.

We might ask ourselves at this point: is this the sort of nemesis that Odysseus encountered on his journey home? Like the Lotus Eaters, we have feasted too long on the wrong food which makes us forget who we are and where we are going. Out of the existential nihilism which is encroaching on us, the Self is responding to this by acceleration in consciousness.

Chapter 11

The Dark Night of the Soul

*You don't choose a dark night for yourself. It is given to you. Your job
is to get close to it and sift it for its gold...*
Thomas Moore

Although St John of the Cross wrote this in the 16th century, it
has even more value today in our modern world than it did then.
The 'Dark Night of the Soul' was comprised of two parts: the
'Dark Night of the Senses', which came first and was a prelude
to the 'Dark Night of the Spirit'. I feel the 'Dark Night of the
Senses' is very real today where our culture constellates around
'having more' and 'becoming more' so that value is placed on
material objects and prestige rather than spirituality and
creativity. Because I feel that many people are undergoing a
'Dark Night of the Senses' rather than a reactive or pathological
depression, I feel it is important to explore the work that St John
of the Cross and Teresa of Avila created together. To understand
the teaching of someone we are interested in we need to understand their story. And particularly, here in this chapter, I want to
look at how extreme deprivation and inner conflict gave birth to
works of great insight and beauty.

When I was 19 and suffering from chronic suicidal
depression, Cathy, a woman I respected very much and who was
a spiritual mentor for me at the time, suggested that I was undergoing a 'Dark Night of the Soul Experience'. She said the
symptoms I was experiencing were outside her experience as a

healer and that I should find someone who had insight into and an understanding of my condition. She warned me against seeking medical intervention in the form of medication that could prove too powerful for my 'sensitive' constitution. She advised me to seek the help of a trustworthy spiritual teacher and suggested several in the US who might be able to help. She maintained that I must be an 'old soul' and that I had a special mission in life to heal people since I had chosen to undergo such a burden of suffering myself.

At the time, I didn't know whether to feel relieved or dismayed by Cathy's advice. At least I felt some respite from seeking medication, all of which I'd found had exacerbated my condition or had such unbearable side effects that I was unable to sustain the course of their duration.

Fortunately, in retrospect, I didn't find a spiritual teacher that could offer any enlightenment on the dark night, other than that I had taken on a heavy weight of karma for some reason or other. I say 'fortunately', because I think then and to a certain extent now, there has been so much misunderstanding and embellishments about the subject that I might have lost all sense of reason and become even further alienated from the world, since depression itself, alienates. Instead, it sent me on a quest to find out what an actual 'Dark Night of the Soul' was. I learned that the 'Dark Night of the Soul' was a condition that besieged various saints and holy men and women. A little later I came across the writing of St John of the Cross and Teresa of Avila.

Heeding Cathy's advice concerning medical intervention was not difficult to do. In the 1970s a medication for depressive conditions, although effective in treating some forms of depression, still had many side effects which made them more of a trial than a relief. Many of them were mind and body numbing with side effects of excessive sedation, trembling, weight gain, notorious dry mouth, constipation and difficulty in urinating. Today, since the advent of SSRI'S, like Prozac and Cipramil, drugs have become more refined and tailored to acting on specific neuro-transmitters (see Chapter 6).

For some years my outlook vacillated between my annual descent into suicidal depression as an ongoing 'Dark Night of the Soul' or a creative darkness which I knew many artistic people underwent. My feelings about myself fluctuated between grandiosity at being such an old soul taking on the world suffering, and feelings of immense shame and self punishment that I was still experiencing a condition that positively crippled me for about six months of the year. When I finally emerged from the depression I felt an inexplicable joy and union with every-thing in the world.

Today, 'Dark Night of the Soul' has become part of the jargon in spiritual, particularly 'new age' circles, where it is used to describe anything from depression, to the loss of a loved one, to a dynamic career change or a midlife crises. And this isn't to undermine the validity of major life events, but to redefine the context and content of a 'Dark Night of the Soul' in a spiritual sense.

To do this we will look into the lives and spiritual practice of these two saints, St Teresa of Avila and St John of the Cross.

Teresa of Avila

Teresa was born in 1515 in the city of Avila, fifty miles west of Madrid. She was born to a wealthy weaving family, and was one of ten children. At the age of twelve her mother died and she was sent to a convent by her father. Although her father wanted her to develop her religious life, he was against her becoming a nun. But it was during her time in the convent, where she struggled against the burgeoning need within her to become a nun, that she became ill and took two years to recover. This was to be the first of many illnesses which were to dog her throughout her life. In psychological terms, this illness could have been the result of her inner struggle between her father's wishes and the call of her destiny. Finally her father relented and Teresa, at the age of twenty, became a Carmelite novice and then a nun.

Shortly after making this commitment, Teresa became victim to an illness that almost killed her and paralyzed her legs for three years. It was by the invocation of St Joseph that she underwent a miraculous healing which was to build a strong foundation for her spiritual life.

Up until the age of fifty we learn little more about St Teresa where we hear she undergoes a long and painful transformation of character after learning that she is suffering from spiritual pride. This is a subtle yet potent condition that many seekers on the spiritual path prey to in their obsession to do their best and do the right thing. Admitting this in herself was to play a crucial part in her psychological understanding of human nature. Simultaneously, her self doubts increased, especially when it came to her spiritual experiences where she felt that she was in communion with God and that He was talking to her. While she was engaged in prayer such communications seemed quite natural, but when held up to the sobering light of day she had fears about their validity and even doubted her sanity.

Seeking the help of her spiritual contemporaries and guides only confirmed her greatest fears of being deluded and that the voices emanated from the Devil. For her, this was the real dark night of her soul; to experience that exquisite presence of God only to be deluged by thoughts of disbelief and failure. But since these experiences didn't go away, she had to make a choice between surrendering to God, where she felt all was well or betray herself time and time again. Although she cut herself off from her spiritual authorities, her experience of God became stronger so that she no longer felt alienated and alone.

It was soon after this deeper commitment to her spiritual inner life that she finally met someone, a Franciscan friar, who was sure of her authenticity and became her trusted colleague and friend. He even went to her spiritual directors and assured them that what she was experiencing was genuine. Although this friar was only to be in her life for two years, during that time he inspired her to become a major reformer of the Carmelite order. This order had been founded in the 12th century in the Palestinian desert where monks and holy men sought prayer and contemplation in the caves on the slopes of Mount Carmel. Over the years, the Carmelite order had changed so that emphasis was placed on community and outward things rather than solitude and contemplation which were key to spiritual development. Teresa was intent on returning the order to its original status, not because she particularly favored austerity, but rather as an effort to instill again the spirit of simplicity and humility to the Carmelite Order.

Meeting with St John of the Cross

It was during the reformation of the Carmelite tradition that Teresa first met St John of the Cross. At the time he was less than half her age, and wanted to join the Carthusian Order: a more austere fraternity, where greater emphasis was placed on solitude, poverty and humility. Teresa persuaded him to become involved in the Carmelite reformation and help found discalced homes for men. Here, they worked together as a complimentary team. Where John had great respect for the validity and importance of her spiritual experiences, Teresa, in turn, valued his intellectual prowess.

Imprisonment, Punishment and Enlightenment

However, Teresa and John's period of time working together wasn't to last, as their reformation fuelled outrage from the church towards them and their work. In this heated process fifty Carmelite nuns were excommunicated and St John of the Cross was imprisoned for refusing to denounce Teresa's work.

Neither John nor Teresa had experienced any degree of ease in their life. Both seemed fated to suffer intolerably: Teresa with her bodily ills which almost killed her and St John with a life of extreme poverty. And yet these seemed to be the very conditions that nurtured and nourished the work they were going to do in life and which would live long after them as a moral and spiritual compass for generations to come. Herein lies a lesson and reminder which, although ageless, speaks to us cogently today. The 'work' that we are born to do is rarely revealed through the 'right' conditions or in a state of harmony, but much more often wrought through deprivation, hardship, sickness and disillusionment – the very conditions our modern world seeks to exile from our direct experience. And yet, even in our modern day myths portrayed through film and fiction, time and time again the forces of light and darkness clash together in order to birth something of real value in the world.

Illness, Miraculous Healing and Spiritual Awakening

Here, first in Teresa's story, we come across the suffering so early in her life in both her own physical illness, the death of her mother and later the ambivalence she had towards her father's disapproval of her becoming a nun. Also, on having insight into her spiritual pride she felt disgust with herself and abandoned for years the idea of praying as if to punish herself further for her weaknesses. This was ironical when prayer was to later become the hallmark of her life's work. Her wisdom and insight into the whole process of prayer was to enlighten and inspire many in their spiritual life and still does today.

Always in the loss of something or someone that we love, there is the gain on another level. In Teresa's case this was a call to her destiny in the form of being sent to a convent by her father who wanted to get her life back on religious track. This was after a spell of being immersed in the temptations of the world and romance when she was a teenager. Although this was all part of the process of growing up and preparing for entry into the mundane world, her father must have sensed on some level that her life's work was to be held within a spiritual framework.

Although the illness that was to plague her adult life was an unwelcome intrusion, it also played a critical part in her initiation into the soul work that was to shape her outer work. Where there is limitation and restriction, the flame of opportunity burns brightly. In fact, it was through her illness that she passed through another portal of initiation. She received a miraculous healing when praying to St Joseph. Energized by the healing, she experienced a call to her destiny.

In psychospiritual terms she received an opening: a direct contact with the Self where there was a spiritual awakening. After being crippled and made an invalid for three years she must have experienced a joyous sense of relief and release as she came into contact with the very real energies of the Self. On a personality level this can have profound implications where the personality attributes the spiritual awakening to itself and the ego becomes inflated. There is often a sense of being special or 'chosen' with the accompanying grandiosity. Alternately, there may be regression to an earlier state of consciousness and a denial of what has happened through fear and lack of understanding. This, in everyday terms, is known as the 'repression of the sublime' and strong levels of denial come to the fore as defense mechanisms which protect the personality from having to pursue a somewhat painful pattern of growth. In time, the experience is relegated to the unconscious and anything that triggers this back into consciousness becomes defended against. This defense or repression of the sublime is at the root of a lot of prejudice, cynicism, hatred and ridicule.

In Teresa's case she was sufficiently grounded to meet the spiritual awakening on the level it presented itself, experiencing it as a 'calling'. But there is a fine line between diligent prayer and obsession. At what point does diligence give way to obsession? When does one's focus become ambitious rather than willing? These are difficult questions to answer because, psychospiritually, many of us are still in the kindergarten consciousness and learning discernment about this. There is nothing wrong with self-discipline, with diligence, with taking pride in one's work, whether it is a spiritual, devotional, mental or physical work. The problem kicks in when pride becomes distorted and we become possessive over what we do. Instead of working from the heart centre, we make a subtle transition to the ego level; we want to do the right thing, to *be right*, rather than let that essence of rightness work through us. Spiritual pride becomes foreground when we decide to take control of our spiritual growth and simultaneously stifle it. The intention to do our best is good, but the moment we apply worldly ambition to the equation it becomes something else. To be fair, it's difficult to know when we have made this transition, or spiritual transgression, because we can feel very good about ourselves and what we are doing. The only criteria to self-test this theory is to check out if we have feelings of being special, or feel morally superior to others.

Ideally, we need a mirror, but the mirror needs to be clean to reflect a clear image. Our friends, even our spiritual directors may not be our best mirrors.

Teresa was fortunate to have a good mirror in her sisters and she had sufficient humility to accept this. After any spiritual awakening there is always the descent, or at least there should be as descent and ground which are necessary in order to integrate the spiritual experience into everyday consciousness. And this is where the hard work comes in because, once we have integrated the experience into our psyche, we can never be quite the same again; we are permanently changed because a veil has been lifted. With this increase in consciousness emerges responsibility and service.

The Importance of Humility
Joseph Campbell, renowned mythologist and university lecturer,

wrote in his book, *Myths to Live by*, about the importance for the hero to have humility in order to contain the vision and success he may have gained on his adventure. If he didn't possess humility the insight he had gained could not have become passed onto his tribe. He would have become too inflated with his own importance to be of service and the tribe would have looked to him as the hero and the savior rather than understanding that they as individuals were capable of treading that same hero's path. In both Teresa's and John's case we can see how humiliation molded the chalice of grace.

The good and bad side of any spiritual awakening is that it casts light upon any defects in our personality that might need adjustment. Because of this we can feel disappointed with the defects of our character and even disgusted, as did Teresa who took it to an extreme so that she cut herself off from her everyday ritual of prayer for many years, feeling she didn't deserve any answers to her prayers. But what this did evoke in her soul was an understanding behind the intention and motive of prayer which she said was '95 percent about desire'. This was a valuable observation that would not have formed if she hadn't questioned her spiritual life.

Her return to prayer was punctuated by ecstatic visions and deep communion with God in which she was urged to give up talking with men and talk to angels instead. While in prayer, she experienced a peace, joy and deep sense of rightness in this contact. But on a mental level she was suspicious of it and worried that she might be imagining it or suffering from delusions of grandeur. When she talked about her visions and experiences to her spiritual directors she was ridiculed and warned that this was the work of the devil. This was Teresa's dark night and here Gerald May defines the 'Dark Night of the Soul' as something mysterious and unknown; an experience that the everyday mind is unable to unravel or come to terms with.

Her meeting with John at the time she was reforming the

Carmelite order was a confirmation of her decision to trust what she was experiencing. These intense periods of spiritual doubt and questioning are all part of the dark night experience. Once a choice has been made deep in the soul to trust the experience, confirmation comes in the form of grace which I will expand on a little later.

St John of the Cross

John, although born from wealthy parentage, was disinherited by them when his father married a poor weaver. He began his life in poverty and soon after his birth his father died leaving his mother and two older brothers destitute. His mother, after losing one of his brothers through malnutrition, sent John to an orphanage school run by the church as she could no longer support him. There he excelled academically and worked in a hospital for the poor as an auxiliary helper before being accepted into a Jesuit school.

His meeting with Teresa was destined in that they shared the same passion and within that context achieved a phenomenal amount of work between them. Shared passion energizes the will and the fact that their joint will was aligned to the Self made their work manifest on a collective level rather than a personal one. Had it not been for his work with Teresa, he may never have been imprisoned and birthed the work for which he was to become so well known.

The reformation of the Carmelite tradition opposed the old order, and it was this that led to St John's imprisonment. But, as we have learned, it was more than imprisonment; it was sustained abuse over a period of time where he was flogged daily, given only bread and water and where he must have felt abandoned by God. This abuse and steady erosion of his self-esteem becomes reminiscent of the sort of profound initiation that heralds the inclusion into any tribal or religious culture where the self-will is broken down in service to the Greater.

Experiences like these might seem pointless and meaningless if we were not to, time and time again, have an insight into what is endeavoring to emerge through the pain. In John's case, where he was subjected to solitary confinement in a small cramped cell with just a slit to let in the light of day, it wasn't the brokenness and the story of abuse that emerged, but instead a poem, *The Spiritual Canticle*. It was a canticle of praise: of love to God, whom he named his Beloved. Through the lens of the world it seems crazy to see how from the depths of deprivation, pain and darkness, love could emerge: a love that would see him through the writing of *The Ascent of Mount Carmel* and *The Living Flame of Love*. The poems themselves are distillations of great beauty and love: an invocation to the Divine. Sadly it is the commentaries around them where he had been asked to explain them that have taken precedence over the poems upon which they are based.

There is something about the nature of imprisonment and deprivation that awakens the flame of the divine in our soul. Kahil Gibran's work, *The Prophet*, reveals 'the pain is the breaking of the shell that encloses our understanding'. This wasn't just so for St John, but also for Dante, John Bunyan and Oscar Wilde in his writing of *De Profundis*. Like the potter's clay, these seminal works fired under great heat and transformed through the gift of grace. I am reminded here of the North American Indian Medicine Wheel tradition and the Medicine Cards that are comprised of the sacred animals which ensouled the medicine. Not all medicine, as we know, is pleasant; in fact, often the best is unpalatable to our refined taste. I am thinking here of the bat who is a denizen of the night and brings about the transformative medicine of rebirth. Bat medicine calls the shaman to death through grueling rituals which assault the body, mind and senses. These rituals are in place to break down all former ideas about the self. In our civilized culture we have all ingested cultural mindsets which give us a sense of place in the world. Initially, these mindsets or beliefs were in place to keep us safe from meddling into affairs that could be detrimental to ourselves and others. In time, these mindsets, instead of being protective, become imprisoning: stifling us so that we are unable to grow any more and reach our potential. Beliefs become habitual to such a degree that part of us, which often presents itself as violent and aggressive, demands that we dislodge them. Something violent and disruptive needs to dislodge them if we are to move forward. Although often grueling, this is a natural process like the storms that root out the old and weak in nature or the hurricanes that reshape landscapes and living communities that exist within them. Although beliefs can be dissolved less violently through time and effort, the process is long and protracted, like the honing smooth of sharp edged stones by the sea. And I think that here we meet the distinction between pathological depression and the 'Dark Night of the Soul' – grace is the key.

Grace

So what is grace?

'Grace is unconditional love,' writes minister, Matthew Fox. 'Grace is about gift.'

But how does this translate into the reality of our normal everyday lives?

Grace, to me, is a re-awakening of love which transforms what appears to be a deeply negative experience to a positive one. The heart surrenders to its pain, and within that surrendering emerges grace.

I remember when I lived on a small island in the Oslo Fjord that had one shop which sold everything. It was owned by a kind and loving man called Ali who had moved from Pakistan with his family. Like anyone from a warm country, he found the climate cold in winter. "But," he would always say. "Whenever I feel low, I think about what I do have instead of what I haven't got."

Thankfully, I have often remembered this when my worldly

mind struggles with rarely having enough money to go on holiday or take a break from work. I have a lot. By some act of grace, I have someone who supports me in what I choose to do. At the moment I have my health which is valuable to anyone with a reoccurring illness and I have a roof over my head. Having been homeless myself I appreciate this too. Having resources and finances does not necessarily confer grace, but the provision of these gifts in a time of economic drought can be experienced as an act of grace.

Energetically, I can experience the shift in my internal dynamics: a letting go, breathing out and breathing in as if up until that point I had stopped breathing. If gratitude and praise unlock the door to grace, grace is, literally, the key. This isn't something that can be written down like a magical formula which can be memorized and practiced. It is a quality that can only be experienced. Neither is it relegated to the domain of spiritual masters, matriarchs and saints. Grace is omnipresent, but it cannot be grasped at or stolen. It is William Blake's 'kissing the joy as it flies'. Grace is transformative. It is magical. It is the fairy god mother in the Grimm's fairy tales that rescues the princess Cinderella from her life of drudgery and the prince that awakens the Sleeping Beauty from her terminal slumber. Grace enters in when all else fails, if we allow it in. The door handle is on our side.

Chapter 12

Defining the Dark Night

Are you willing to be sponged out, erased, cancelled?
Made nothing?
Are you willing to be made nothing?
Dipped into oblivion?
If not, you will never really change...
D H Lawrence

In this chapter I want to give structure to the 'Dark Night of the Soul' by addressing its two components: 'Dark Night of the Senses' and 'Dark Night of the Spirit'. By exploring these and looking at both their active and passive elements, I hope to unpack their qualities and what they mean for us in this day and age.

It seems ironical that in order for the light to enter us, we have to surrender to darkness greater than we have ever known. We cannot understand this within the language of the world until we see how light is intimately bound with darkness; the stars are only visible at night. In the natural world the seeds germinate within the depth of the earth: their dark womb. Our world is divided into night and day, the winter solstice, the summer solstice, conscious and unconscious, visible and invisible, knowable and unknowable. Light and dark are not so much polar opposites, but complimentary parts of the same continuum. Likewise, humans who have freewill are capable of manifesting the highest good as well as the darkest evil.

What is unconscious within us becomes uncomfortable at the point at which it begins to become conscious. And as consciousness dawns, we experience the acute pain of birth and the light that brings consciousness is almost a radiance comparable with the darkness when it was unconscious.

Although, in everyday language, a 'Dark Night of the Soul' may be defined loosely as a period of inner spiritual darkness, it is more than that. For example, St John of the Cross's graphic writings about the dark night intimate at the very real experience of love: divine love that emerges and persists through such a time. His work is an intensely beautiful and intimate account of his love affair with God, the Beloved. He only has good things to say about the dark night, but he admits that this is only after one has passed through an often grueling interior struggle and surrendered to the process. St John of the Cross made very clear distinctions between the stages of a dark night experience, in the form of *active* and *passive* components and the quality of the dark nights. These he also referred to as passive and active purgation. He believed that the 'Dark Night of the Soul' can be divided into the 'Dark Night of the Senses' and the 'Dark Night of the Spirit'. These I am going to approach individually and in the form they usually manifest. The first, 'Dark Night of the Senses', involves a purgation or deep cleansing of the soul. The second is the 'Dark Night of the Spirit'.

Dark Night of the Senses

The night of sense is common and comes to many: these are the beginners; and of this night we shall speak first... The first purgation or night is bitter and terrible to sense, as we shall now show.
St John of the Cross

St John of the Cross believed the 'Dark Night of the Senses' was experienced by many and was an absolutely crucial initiation into the life of the spirit. The whole nature of this dark night is to prepare the way for the 'Dark Night of the Spirit', although he makes it clear that the 'Dark Night of the Spirit' is rarer and may not manifest until many years after the 'Dark Night of the Senses', if at all.

He defined the latter as a period of withdrawal from the pleasures of the senses. The things that brought happiness and pleasure before, no longer capture us. Our senses, the windows to the world, appear to be withdrawn. This closing down of participatory enjoyment in the objects of the world is the first stage in turning away from material values. And although other distractions and pleasures may be sought, they are somehow eclipsed by a darkening of the senses. Within the loss is always the opportunity. And the nature of the darkening of the senses is to free us from our attachment to material objects.

Because we have forgotten who we are in our descent from God, the part of us that still remembers the perfection and beauty, glimpses images of it in the world, images that we quickly idolize. As Robert May says; 'We give them our time, energy, and attention whether we want to or not'. The objects become our idols rather than a metaphor for something deep within the soul with which we have lost touch. We will find that many of the things we becomes addicted to, whether patterns of behavior or objects, give us a pale link with the divine we have lost. In a world of objects we become obsessed with attaining the objects, more of them, instead of – as British poet, Blake, poetically intimated – 'kissing the joy as it flies'. Once we possess the object, the essence that animated it quickly vanishes and it sits on the shelf forgotten until we become captured by the next glittering bauble. The ironical thing is that in the language of the spirit, the moment we try to possess something, it vanishes or dies. Like the beautiful rose we pick and place in a vase; it has already begun to die.

All of us have a deep desire to be free, to walk free from our obsession with possessing, having and holding. The 'Dark Night of the Senses' provides us with the opportunity. Until this opportunity manifests we believe that it is the objects themselves and the acquisition of wealth that makes us free.

St John refers to the value of the 'Dark Night of the Senses' in the spiritual beginner where diligent prayer and exercises may give rise to a secret pride: of being spiritually superior to others. Besides spiritual pride there may be spiritual gluttony and avarice where there is greed in possessing many books and attending numerous spiritual counsels in an effort to make one spiritually superior to others. St John warns of this in his teachings. Matthew Fox supports this: 'True humility is a journeying into the darkness of oneself... If we can face the darkness within, we can face the darkness that is God.'

Again, these deep appetites and desires that are masquerading under the guise of spirituality, are often more difficult to rid oneself of than material sensual pleasures as their attraction is more subtle and cunning. Again and again, he emphasizes that the way that one moves from beginners on the path to disciples who are beginning to contemplate the divine, is through humility. Spiritual pride is the greatest enemy here. He speaks also of spiritual luxuries in the form of expensive trinkets and relics which invite dark subtle attachments and incite envy in others.

Active Night of the Senses
The active night of the senses is marked by a sustained and focused period of turning inward through activities such as prayer, meditation, yoga, breathing, writing journals and going on retreats. As the worldly senses have become eclipsed by a darkness that takes the enjoyment out of sensual pleasure, the concentration becomes focused on developing other aspects of the self. This active period can easily fill any existential emptiness and disillusionment with the world. Since the whole

object of the dark night is to call the individual to deeper union with God, spiritual activities appear to be the only apparatus that works for the individual. Walks in nature, running, sailing, mountain climbing and canoeing which waken the spirit to beauty and a sense of the sacred, can be experienced too. Periods of fasting may be experienced as a way of purifying the body. Restraint and self-discipline are useful tools in developing this link with the world of spirit. All these activities are performed consciously and evoked by the personal will.

As concentration develops and the spiritual practice stabilizes the inner restlessness, the disciple may experience the inflowing of a profound sense of wellbeing and peace. He or she can experience closeness to God that they have never known before and a sense of deep rightness within their being. As time goes by and the student's spiritual practice deepens, a subtle transition in priorities takes place between the material world that claimed the senses and the inner world which links the soul to meaning, purpose and values.

This period of deepening is one that meditation teacher and psychologist Jack Kornfield refers to in his book, *A Path with a Heart*. In Theravada Buddhism there is a 'map of the elders' which is used to describe various meditative states of concentration. The first of these states is called 'The Realms of Absorption'. This is where the spiritual practitioner, through the process of concentration, repetition and surrender, begins to undergo a steadily deepening state of consciousness which includes rapture and happiness, even joy. These four levels of absorption, accessed through concentration and practice, can be reached through visualization exercises that reflect upon color or form, or through the breath. During this process the student may feel as though they are in union with the Gods. Beyond these states are realms of formless absorption where the student may access and develop various psychic abilities such as telepathy and telekinesis.

The subtle trap underlying the acquisition of these states of consciousness is the illusion that one has reached enlightenment or begun craving for ever higher states of consciousness. The personality can become just as addicted to spiritual expansion as to drugs which invoke the senses, as do food and sex. If resting in these states of absorption becomes an escape from dealing with the world of matter, then it verges on becoming an addiction that is hard to break. It is for this reason that the 'Dark Night of the Spirit' comes into being, ushering one's experience onto an ever deepening connection with God.

Passive Night of the Senses

Here, the passive night of the senses isn't about prayer and meditation since these tools no longer work at this stage. Instead, quietness is needed in the soul and a sense of waiting on God, the Beloved. Within this context there is a subtle transition between being in communication with God through the medium of the senses to the medium of the spirit.

Grace may come in the loosening of bonds, a letting go of long cherished objects of comfort and a surrendering to the process. On the other hand, further liberation can be painful as we are stripped of layer upon layer of defense that protects us from our vulnerability. Here, even prayer, meditation and the church or mosque lose their appeal. People, who have maintained a rigorous practice of prayer and meditation for years, may actually give them up during this part of the deepening.

Gerald May talks about the obscurity around this process. If we try to understand it, it eludes us. If we let go of the confusion around not being able to articulate and understand our experience a burgeoning trust begins to form in its place.

It is important to focus on the nature of the dark night, to bring one closer to the Divine, to Love. Love's ways do not respond to the formula of the senses any more than they do to the mind and will. Feelings of self doubt are natural here and rather than indicating that something is wrong, indicate that something is *actually right!*

The 'Dark Night of the Senses' is a relentless hollowing out of the soul so that it is empty and arid enough to contain the fire of the Spirit. This then is the often long and arduous preparation for the 'Dark Night of the Spirit'.

Dark Night of the Spirit

The night of the spirit is the portion of very few, and these are they
that are already practiced and proficient, of whom we shall treat
hereafter... The second night bears no comparison with it (the first
night) for it is horrible and awful to the spirit...
St John of the Cross

The single most debilitating factor about the 'Dark Night of the Spirit' is the feeling of being abandoned by God. This can be experienced as a deep betrayal, a punishment and a crucifixion. This sense of abandonment and betrayal rarely happens overnight. It is a gradual process occurring over weeks, months, even years, accompanied by a deep sense of exasperation, frustration and helplessness. Just as the 'Dark Night of the Senses' began with an increasing sense of disillusionment with the world and all its distractions, so is this second night accompanied by a failure to find satisfaction in all the spiritual tools of development that worked before. It is like finding the well worked magical wand that could produce different states of being before, wholly impotent. It is no surprise that St John of the Cross referred to the night of the spirit as the night of faith. Faith is needed to keep on keeping on when the doors to heaven seem closed and one is met by an all-pervading sense of aridity and emptiness. As this disillusionment continues, the initiate may decide to abandon the spiritual path and return to the ways of the world, until a deepening sense of inner impoverishment calls him back to practice again. It must be remembered that God has not abandoned the initiate but is 'calling' him onto a deeper level of commitment and unity. This is not unlike the adult birds no longer feeding their young so that the fledglings are hungry enough to respond to their parent's invitation and become fledged outside the nest. The 'Dark Night of the Spirit' is all about subtraction, dissolution, death and decay. In nature, it corresponds to the stripping stage of the fall where, in the midst of great color and majesty, these same leaves are stripped from the tree, laying the branches bare to another turn of the cycle through rebirth in the spring.

One of the temptations during the sense of estrangement from God's kingdom is to redouble ones efforts in a frenzied attempt to win back that contact with God again. But like being in quagmire, the more one struggles to do this, the deeper becomes the sense of being cut off and imprisoned from the former splendor.

May refers to the 'Dark Night of the Spirit' as being 'like midnight, a deeper darkness in which all things are obscured'. Where the 'Dark Night of the Senses' is primarily about sensory pleasures and gratifications, the night of the spirit is about thought forms, the intellect, the mind and memory. Finding long held beliefs that served us well and formed our worldview of reality are crumbling, can be deeply unsettling. Our sense of our self and the world is breaking down. And this gradual disso-lution is reflected in revelations in our everyday dealings with others, where we might discover truths about our friends and colleagues that rock us to the core. Within breakdown is the opportunity for *breakthrough* of whole new structures and ways of being. Our model of the world is changing.

St John further divides the 'Dark Night of the Spirit' into passive and active elements. Basically, the active element is about effort, doing and making something happen. The passive element is more about grace and the miraculous, where effort and the concept of doing only impede the process. The overriding component of this second dark night is a sense of being in a 'fog'; of everything being obscure and indefinite. The doubts that are entertained here about what is real and what isn't real, true and untrue serve to eliminate the mindset that we had built up in an effort to keep us safe. This is all about letting go.

Active Night of the Spirit

How, although this night brings darkness to the spirit, it does so in order to illumine it and give it light.
St John of the Cross

John refers here to the practicing of the virtues of faith, hope and love, but warns against becoming fixated by them in wanting to do the 'right thing' which can become a preoccupation in itself. The intellect, memory and will need to be emptied rather than focused, as focusing and concentration give rise to more content. He encourages a dispassionate attitude to insights and images however profound they may be. Again he urges continuity of moderation and restraint. The whole focus is on simplifying the mind, allowing it to become receptive and childlike rather than dissecting, amassing and analyzing.

According to Kornfield's map of the elders this 'Dark Night of the Spirit' corresponds to the second state of meditative consciousness. In contrast to the absorption of the first dark night where there was a steady expansion, the night of the spirit is about subtraction and dissolution. The initiate moves from the expansive telescopic lens of consciousness to the microscopic lens of looking at the body and mind, the motives, the desires, the limitations. An observing component is brought into play, one that bears witness without judgment, without becoming caught up in a condition.

Both the active nights of the senses and spirit are preparation for the real inner work. St John urges that unless the soul is 'filled with deeper more urgent longings', all one's efforts are wasted. The passive night is a way of deepening the process, gravitating to the 'centre of the soul' which St John refers to as God. Both he and Teresa stress that we cannot do it on our own. No amount of self-will and dedication can instigate this process, what is required is a surrendering to Grace. It is through both the 'Dark Night of the Senses and the Spirit' that a longing is awoken in the soul for union with God. The longing is there all the time, but is unconscious and is behind our longing for union with another. When we are in love with another it is not so much a matter of looking through rose-tinted glasses, but perceiving the divine in the other through the lens of the spirit.

Passive Night of the Spirit
St John describes this to be principally about one's relationship with God. Always our relationship with the 'other' is reflected in our relationship with ourselves. If our relationship with ourselves changes, as it does in this long process, then our relationship with God changes too. In psychological language, what happens intrapsychically is mirrored extrapsychically. We may experience a sense of loss, of having been abandoned by God as our mindsets erode and fragment. But emerging through this wasteland is a new sense of God. This renewed sense of God may remind us of what we held as a child and somehow lost in the process of growing up and becoming worldly. Through the purifying process of the dark night we perceive God as a God of compassion, of love, rather than one of punishment and retribution as dictated by the older proponents of the church.

Like all interior processes, the dark night is non-linear and very often cyclical, appearing through the strands of life's fabric and forming the backcloth of its rich tapestry. Like anything natural, it is organic and subject to waxing and waning of the seasons. The dark night is an intimate and ongoing relationship with God. 'This dark night,' St John says, 'is an inflow of God in the soul.'

One never stops being in relationship with the Divine. It is only our perception of this that changes. The 'Dark Night of the Spirit' is about union with the Divine, of which the 'Dark Night of the Senses' has been the forerunner. As in the 'Dark Night of the Senses' an appetite has been awakened for the spiritual life; the loss and divestment of the qualities it offers gives rise to a deeper longing for God. It is this longing to experience union with the Divine that opens the heart to surrender to the dying process, the inner crucifixion which heralds a rebirth.

Chapter 13

Depression and the Dark Night of the Soul

Depression is a psychological sickness; a dark night is a spiritual trial.
Thomas Moore

I have researched extensively into the symptoms and defining factors between various types of depressive disorder and dark night experiences and although there are some clear distinctions they exist along the same continuum. The table at the end of this chapter clarifies some of these differences and distinctions.

It is no more possible to isolate spirit from pathology than it is to isolate spirit from matter, since spirit is the tributary which connects and runs through all life. A deep depression may seriously undermine one's previous perspective of life to such a degree that a whole new career direction is called for and a former atheist may become a diligent follower of a religious faith. Any experience that breaks up the foundations of what we held to be true, whether it is in the form of depression, bereavement or a heart attack, may open the door to seeking spiritual meaning in our life. A deep depression is potentially as life threatening as any other organic illness. Although in the time of St John of the Cross and Teresa of Avila, a 'Dark Night of the Soul' was seen as an integral part of a spiritual disciple's life, it took place more in isolation from the world than depression does. Today, we may not be imprisoned for our beliefs and be socially isolated on a geographical level, but still feel imprisoned by our circumstances and isolated on an existential level. It may be impossible for us to know whether we are going through a spiritual dark night or struggling with a pathological illness.

Every experience in life, however difficult and harrowing, holds the potential for the Self to emerge. The Self is omnipresent, and obviously the more spiritual awareness one has, the more a period of depression can be part of a dark night experience. Psychiatrist, Robert May believes that very often a deep depression can happen at the same time as a dark night.

But herein there are dangers of avoiding psychological growth and insight by passing a depressive disorder off as solely a dark night and only dealing with it on that level, if at all. This is known as a 'spiritual cop-out'. Similarly, a dark night experience may be interpreted solely on a psychological level and regarded as something related to personal history to be transformed and cured. We cannot understand the dark night experience on a purely psychological level as we cannot understand depression purely on a spiritual level. For this reason depression and dark night experiences need to be held in a psychospiritual context, otherwise support and guidance are at their best limited, and at their worst can be dangerous.

For years I struggled against medication as I believed that there was something intrinsically wrong with taking it. I had a mindset which held rigidly to the belief that taking medication was wrong because it interfered with God's process. Many of the people I was involved with supported this belief and affirmed that I was taking on 'difficult karma', and that I was doing this for the world. Part of me believed that I was experiencing an ongoing 'Dark Night of the Soul', and another part of me believed that I was suffering from psychological damage from an extremely traumatic childhood. The part of me that believed it was a 'Dark Night of the Soul' came from the place within me that knew great joy and a sense of union with the Divine when I finally, after months, emerged from the darkness. In one sense, I felt spiritually abandoned by God in depression because when I wasn't depressed I felt a deep connection to God. After emergence I experienced a profound joy and sense of union and a great love opening in my being. As much as I hated the darkness, the pain and misery, I was equally afraid of losing the light, that sense of joy too, and in a way this stopped me from seeking therapy. Additionally, as a writer and poet, I was afraid of losing my creativity. This is a very real fear experienced by many creative people.

When I finally made a decision to seek psychiatric advice,I was led to just the right psychiatrist who acknowledged my childhood history and my spiritual outlook, but diagnosed me with bipolar disorder and put me on an effective SSRI rather than lithium. She felt my highs weren't too high. If anything, the medication enabled me to experience a more normal life so that I relaxed my ambivalence to medical intervention. If you have a painful illness you accept the treatment, you don't struggle with 'maybe this is going to interfere with God's process'. You take the medication because your life depends on it. And 'yes', medications can be on a roller coaster of things working, and then failing to work and side effects. A lot of the fear of taking medication can be due to some of the earlier drugs that have been used in psychiatric medicine with their numbing and sedative side effects, but it can also be part of a spiritual or mental arrogance, about doing the right thing. St John writes about the problem of spiritual directors who have not had suffi-cient insight into their own nature, meeting a chronic depression that requires medical intervention as a dark night experience or, worse, a punishment for karmic wrongs. The problem is in inter-pretation and exclusion. If a symptom is only interpreted from a psychological perspective and its biological and spiritual component edited out, this creates an imbalance. Exclusion always invites limitation in a negative way that translates as prejudice towards anything that threatens its supremacy.

Prejudice is based on an intrinsic fear of being eclipsed by something greater; being swallowed up in something we have no control over. On a spiritual level it translates as a fear of not doing the right thing, of failing and of falling. On a psychological level, there is a fear of the unknown, of seeming powerlessness. Supposing, after all these years, psychology and psychotherapy have to admit that everything they held true about depression is no longer true and they have to start again. Psychotherapist, James Hillman, has effectively admitted this in his book, *We've had a Hundred Years of Psychotherapy and the World isn't getting Any Better*. On the biological level there is a fear of losing control, of being powerless...

But, ironically, admitting our own powerlessness, invites a different sort of power to become manifest, whether our role be one of patient, doctor or healer.

The 'Dark Night of the Soul', through the senses and the spirit, describes an ancient process that happens throughout our world cultures. St John talks about the necessary purgation before the ascent: to go down before we go up. If we just ascend, we set ourselves up for a grave. The descent to hell and purgation which is clearly defined in Dante's *Divine Comedy*, occurs when the protagonist was taken by his guide, Virgil, to hell then up into purgatory where the inhabitants were able to redeem themselves through suffering before they were able to enter paradise. The age old cycle is exemplified in nature, where the growth of the tree is primarily downward before we can see it emerging through the soil. Without roots, something to anchor us, we perish like the mythological Icarus whose waxen wings melted because he flew too close to the sun. We can see this cyclical process of purgation and stripping in nature when the strong fall winds tear the leaves from the trees along with any weak branches. The onslaught of these elements can seem relentless, yet we accept them as necessary to the cyclical process.

The table I include in this section will, hopefully, prove useful as a checklist in determining some of the symptomatic differences between a 'Dark Night of the Soul' and pathological depression.

Distinctions between Dark Night of the Soul and Pathological Depression

Dark Night of The Soul	Pathological Depression
Loss of interest in activities that normally bring pleasure	Desperate clutching onto objects and people.
Existential emptiness	Emotional deadness
Feelings of being alone	Desperate loneliness
A desire to turn within and away from the world	Fear of being isolated.
Need to find a spiritual director/guide	Drive to find a 'fix-it' remedy
A sense of being abandoned by God	A feeling of being punished by God
Prayer and meditation no longer bring solace	Exile from God
Breaking down of belief systems	Breakdown of mind and emotions
A need to let go – let God/radical trust	Cannot trust
A sense of rightness	Something deeply wrong
Peace. A sense that all is well	Deep anxiety, fear and dread
Confusion/not knowing	Desperate need to find reasons for dis-ease
Compassion for others that are suffering	Unable to consider others
Feelings of profound sadness interspersed with deep joy	Obsessional thoughts/ fragmented thought

Thoughts of death and mortality	Thoughts of self-harm/suicidal
Ability to maintain a sense of self, despite confusion and difficulty	Loss of sense of self. Feelings of being overwhelmed
Ability to carry on with daily life; work and relationships	Difficulty on holding down a job and sustaining relationships

Chapter 14

Treasure and Creative Darkness

If you give birth to what is inside you,
What is inside you will set you free.
If you do not give birth to what is inside you,
what is inside you will destroy you.

Anon

There is a type of depression which corresponds with the creative process (see Chapter 2). Although a creative idea may emerge effortlessly, the work involved in grounding the insight and bringing it into matter is not so simple; it involves trust, creative darkness and frustration. Many potentially creative people, who have little understanding of how the creative process works, give up easily and perhaps, as a result, descend into a deeper depression.

I had originally intended that this chapter follow on the heels of the Persephone myth, but it didn't seem to fit until I remembered that treasure always lies at the end of the journey. In fact, bearing in mind the skills that are needed in this work of soul-making, it is better that the whole idea of treasure is put to one side, for it is the journey which is important. As long as this is remembered then the treasure will come without overtly seeking it.

There has long been an idea that many creative people suffer from madness or depression. Although this is obviously true, in many cases, this can actively discourage people from expressing their creativity. I would like to suggest that creativity is a highly effective way of managing depressive illness which is, by its debilitating nature, potentially destructive. In a sense, it is an act of transformation where the 'I' can become a servant to the Self by aligning to purpose, meaning and values and harnessing powerful energies in such a way that they serve both the individual and humanity.

"So, Dr Kramer, what would have happened if Kierkegaard had taken Prozac?" psychiatrist and author of *Listening to Prozac* was asked at one of his seminars.

Such a compelling question can be applied to a multitude of highly gifted and creative geniuses in the past. Maybe if Prozac had been around in the 19th century, Van Gogh wouldn't have lived out his dramatic life in service of the art that would only really become a classic when he was dead. Maybe Existentialism, which was modeled on the work of Danish philosopher, Kierkegaard, who was deeply suicidal and melancholic, may have never come into being. Maybe Prozac would have rescued Virginia Woolf or Sylvia Plath from the tragedy of premature suicidal death. Yet, even more compelling is the theory that these outstanding people, who struggled with agonizing depths of pain, and in some cases ecstasy, would never have produced anything of worth if they had had a more stable emotional life. Within this framework, creativity and genius has become entwined with suicidal depression, mental instability and the sacred. Our tortured individuals throughout history have become romanticized under the call of their creative work and, because of this are sacrosanct.

Kramer responds to the question with: "The 'what if', rested on a concern that amelioration of depression might cloud a person's moral clarity or dampen a divine spark." He further suggests; 'Depression is more than an illness – it has a sacred aspect.' He believes that the popularity in maintaining this belief was a throwback to when melancholia was romanticized and seen as a fundamental prerequisite to creativity, depth and wisdom. If depressive conditions are sacred, then can we say that all illness has a sacred aspect because suffering gives us an opportunity to find renewed purpose, meaning and value in our inner lives?

Kramer, who writes very movingly about depression in his latest book, *Against Depression*, argues favorably in defense of pharmacological medication in the treatment of depression alongside psychotherapy and counseling. His work has brought him close to the despair and anguish of depressives and his research and understanding of the biological and hereditary components which underpin depression is impressive. He also cites that 'There is an impressive surfeit of depressives who are no more especially talented than the average'.

But, as is often the case, a soul that is destined to enact a major contribution to society often has more than their fair share of inner and outer obstacles to contend with. Opposition and difficulty strengthen the soul. We can see this from Rachel Carson's enormous efforts that went into demystifying science, Madame Curie's determination to continue her research into radium despite illness secondary to her research, and Dr Edward Bach's persistence to carry out his 'alternative' work with Flower Essences in the face of ridicule and exile from his medical contemporaries. Dante, John Bunyan and Oscar Wilde were imprisoned for various reasons and in their imprisonment produced 'great works' that have long outlived them and burn just as brightly today as they did when they first wrote them.

But depression, it is true, does seem to have underpinned a lot of creative work. And, quite frankly, although Prozac, at the time of writing this, has been in existence for nearly twenty years, depression is still rampant in all countries throughout the world. 40,000 thousand people still kill themselves every year in the States alone, and this isn't because of the inefficacy of Prozac to provide relief. People still have free will and medicine, however great its publicity, doesn't work the same in everyone, that is why we have so many brands of drugs available.

Depression runs through every walk of life, not just those who are artistically gifted. Besides Churchill, there was Abraham Lincoln who suffered from debilitating depression. Lincoln, the 16th president of the USA, was a much loved president because he spoke from his heart and managed to touch the hearts of others. But he hadn't started out as a depressed man. On the contrary, he was described as a young man with a sunny and engaging nature. A witty conversationalist, his energy, enthusiasm and ambition won him many admirers. Yet, at twenty-six he was to have his first depressive breakdown, which is a normal age for the onset of unipolar depression. Despite this setback, he managed to command the admiration of his close friends who took it in turns to keep 'suicide watch' when he was dangerously ill.

Although depression was to run like a fault line through his family, affecting both his mother and father, it also surfaced frequently throughout his life, undermining his confidence, making him thin and gaunter than ever.

As a young man, after witnessing a slave being sold, he was so stirred up by its inhumanity that he was to spend a lot of his life working towards abolishing the oppressive practice from the States. This won him friends as well as enemies. Slavery pierced the core of his belief system: that all men and women in the eyes of God were equal. In the midst of his depression he continued to fight to abolish slavery. Seized by a mission which fuelled a deep sense of purpose in life, he fought hard for their freedom. Perhaps, in a sense, this life of oppression lived out by the Africans was an inner metaphor for how oppressed and imprisoned Lincoln felt within himself.

Although he could be hard on himself, Lincoln bore his illness with dignity. When asked about it, he replied "it was unfortunate to suffer from depression, but it was not a failure."

Although his zealous endeavors to implement these laws began to bear fruit, Lincoln was not to see the result of all his passionate fighting because he was assassinated just before this happened. His assassin, one of his enemies, was as much for slavery and repression as Lincoln was against it. I include one of Lincoln's last speeches here as it creates a clear picture of this man's great humanity and vision despite his so often tortured state of mind.

With malice toward none, with charity for all; with firmness in the right, as God gives us to see the right, let us strive on to finish the work we are in; to bind up the nation's wounds; to care for him who shall have borne the battle, and for his widow, and his orphan—to do all which may achieve and cherish a just, and a lasting peace, among ourselves, and with all nations.

What then is the connection between creativity and depression?

Perhaps this compelling question can be answered by looking more closely at the creative process, the implications of allowing it in and also defending ourselves against it on an individual and collective level.

Because creativity is an active organic process, where what is within forces its way out into form, it is far from being a comfortable experience. In nature we can see the old form, whether it is the bud, the seed or the bulb, has to break down in some way as it surrenders to the process which shapes its next stage. We know from empirical experience of childbirth that it isn't easy. It is labor and it is painful. Having the vision of what is to be born or conceived is one thing, but suffering the gap between what is conception and birth is immensely frustrating. In short, no one sets out to be creative out of choice. Being creative is living with the discomfort of the unknown, and being vulnerable in order to be receptive. It is risky because the actual process bridges a huge divide between the familiar, the safe and known and the wild and unfamiliar.

In our fast paced culture, we keep creativity at a distance with the frequent excuse that we don't have time to create, and yet we remain fascinated with creativity. Similarly, we talk about being creative without really understanding what that is or what is involved.

To understand how our cultural and societal attitudes towards creativity are reflected in the world, we only have to look at our relationship with nature. In essence, the natural organic environment is tantamount to creativity and that is why I have modeled the creative process on this. Primarily, the creative process is, in fact, the force of creation. It is the sea in whose depth a life, almost unseen, lives out its existence: from the sap in the trees, to the breadth and infinity of space. It is, in short, terrifyingly awesome and wondrous. This sea of creativity that carries us along, sweeps us through the portals of life and death. The experience that unites the two is a force that we as individuals are powerless to control or halt for any length of time. Amidst absolute carnage and degradation new life-forms push their way into being, whether we have invited them or not; mushrooms push through tarmac, plants and shrubs through the ruined buildings of the past. And in the midst of going to seed and decaying, new life in the form of spores and seeds are carried on the wind to create new life, another cycle.

Basically, we are talking about the life force of which we are a miniscule and integral part, as individuals and as a race. The worst thing we can do is try to stand in the way of this creative force or block it out by going unconscious to it. By blocking out this natural force we injure ourselves and cut ourselves off from our source; we become impoverished and filled with dis-ease. More than anything, we become depressed, repressed and oppressed. I do believe that the collective depression that many of us carry is the result of our closing the door to the life force that brought us into being and shapes our destiny.

A friend and gifted artist, Hanne Jahr, writes of her insight into the creative force when she visited The White Eagle Lodge in Liss, Hampshire, twenty years ago:

Participants at the Sunday Service were invited to come to the retreat house for a discussion following a reading on a certain theme. Although I cannot remember the theme itself, what led up to the experience was White Eagle's writing on a coming new age of peace and brotherhood. One of the participants was expressing his doubt as to whether a new age of brotherhood would happen and the likelihood of being faced with our own destruction instead.

At this point I had what I can only describe as a flash of intuitive insight. I was suddenly raised in consciousness to the level of my higher self. On this level, I felt and became conscious of what I can only describe as the 'Creative Force of the Universe.' I 'saw' that this Creative Force was so much stronger than us. There were people trying to hurry the process along, and many more trying to stop it by 'putting a spanner in the works', so to speak. Yet, I saw, that it made no real difference to the Creative Force. It only brought unhappiness, frustration and stress to those out of harmony with the Creative Force. I realized then that creation goes on despite of us, as well as for us, and the best we can do is to attune ourselves to this force and try to work in cooperation and harmony with it.

And I knew, in relationship to our topic, that the new age of brotherhood would come. But how and in what manner it would be achieved was entirely up to us.

Clues as to how we relate to creativity are to be found in the way in which we respond to nature. Sadly, many of us can not, do not, or have forgotten how to respond. But the arising critical symptoms that are taking place in our global climate such as deforestation, pollution and the disappearance of animals and bees is an urgent invitation from nature to reconnect with this part of ourselves.

Psychologist, James Hillman's words echo this, 'We keep ourselves busy as a manic defense against what we have done to nature...' Further, perhaps we are keeping ourselves busy in an effort to ward off the creative process that is ever endeavoring to come into form within our psyche. We fear that if we stop we will give birth to what? Our dreams surely. For what else can keep us as desperately unhappy as the continual crushing and termination of our dreams? Our mantra in this day and age is, 'I haven't got time...' But what haven't we got time for? It is as if we haven't got time for life. Yet life happens while we are running away from it!

Now that I have written about the discomfort and the struggle of the creative process, I feel I have deflated a number of idyllic and romantic myths around it. And yet, the romance and idealism, joy and ecstasy are all very much part of the creative process as is the agony; for creativity is the agony and the ecstasy; you cannot have one without the other. Contra to the 'either/or' culture we live in, these polar opposites are symbiotic, just as the seeds of decay from the fallen flower heads contain the seeds of new life. The vast blind spot that controls our current belief system is that we have to have one quality and annihilate the opposite quality. We want all the good things in life – longevity, happiness, success and wealth – without putting in any of the groundwork. Until the exiled and divided opposites of our make-up are invited back into our consciousness we will always remain fragmented and fear the very thing that will set us free.

Creativity as Process
Because the creative act is essentially a spontaneous instinctive process, working under the province of the right side of the brain,

which is non-linear, and belonging to the abstract mind, it is difficult to step outside the creative process and define what is taking place.

It was the work of several scientists who were responsible for creating a framework for creativity born from their own experiences. At the end of the 19th century, Herman Helmholtz, a German physicist and scientist, suggested that there were three distinct stages in the creative act. These were the *saturation* of research and amassing information, followed by the second stage of *incubation*, which is mulling over what has been learned. This is concluded by *illumination* which is the sudden insight which comes unbidden.

A few years later, a fourth stage was added to the process by Henri Poncaire, the French mathematician. This he referred to as verification which involved committing the solution to concrete form by testing it out and thus aiding its solidification.

It wasn't until over 50 years later, in 1960, when a fifth stage was added by American Psychologist, Jacob Getzels, which he claimed preceded the initial saturation stage. This was the *first insight*, a mixture of problem finding and problem solving, and a preparatory stage.

When I was doing my MA in psychosynthesis, one of my tutors, Roger Evans, who had co-written a book, *The Creative Manager*, with Peter Russell, used an updated creative model in his work in training business managers. These stages are *preparation*, which supplants the *first Insight*, followed by *frustration*, *incubation*, *insight* and *working out*. Although not hugely different from the original model, I find the inclusion of the frustration phrase very helpful indeed, because that stage of 'stuck- ness', of wondering whether I have it all wrong or have deluded myself, is such an integral part of my own creativity. It also serves to eliminate the mindsets around creativity that it happens without effort or thought. And this is the very mindset that prevents people from following through their own process. After the initial insight, which fuels the imagination and activates passion, along come the usual blockages and frustration which test the strength of the vision.

The Necessity of Frustration

After the snuffing out of the creative fire with cold water, if we don't understand what is happening, we abort our efforts and adhere to a self- defeating belief that we are not creative. But with the creative mantle come frustration and a sense of being embedded in concrete that tests and challenges our strength of commitment. After all, the creative act is a relationship, albeit with something intangible, but relationship it is. And all relationships test us and force us to grow. From the idyllic romance that falls naturally into marriage, the previously unseen thorns in the beautiful rose of earthly love makes itself known, forcing us to change, bend with the wind or against it so that we lose branches and initiate new unplumbed depths within our make-up.

Frustration is as organic as the bud that both longs and fears to break. It is the very force that births determination and endurance and hones the initial floundering attempts to success and perfection. It is the aura that the craftsman, artist, explorer and pioneer wears that draws us irresistibly to their individual truth. It is the fire that melts and shapes the glassblower's work.

Without frustration there is no drive to break through the membrane that encloses our limitation, forcing us onto new levels of brilliance. Frustration, although greatly maligned in our instant production and success obsessed culture, is a vital jewel within. as the grain of sand is to the shining pearl within the oyster. We need to allow the frustration, because in allowing it, we facilitate the process to be birthed through us: a process borne not in our time, but creative time which works against our mechanical time ruled culture.

There are two types of pain in the creative process, I have found. One is the holding back and denying of what longs to be birthed. The other is the creative darkness which is largely about the unknown and untravelled. Not giving birth to what is inside us; the pain of not giving birth to our dreams can push our whole system into breakdown. The foundations of our being begin to crack and fragment and, psychologically, we may experience this as the unconscious beginning to break through. Without a strong enough 'I' to enable us to detach from the process, we become overwhelmed by the experience which can give rise to psychotic episodes and psychic phenomena. This is the presence of the polar opposite of creativity – the destructive side. Only then is a breakthrough possible along with the new insight and rebirth it can offer.

The creative darkness trusts the unknown, which is a lot easier in theory than practice! For each one of us the unknown will present itself in a different way. Vision and knowing can only come through surrendering to the unknown. Although it may not be possible to carry out this alone, it can be enabled by a guide in the form of a therapist, counselor or priest: someone who can, principally, hold the boundaries and act as a transitory foundation until a new one emerges.   Here, I recall again those lines of a film that have stayed with me: *The pain that travels with us the love we hold back.*

The creative act is an act of love, a coupling with a reality greater than ourselves, a union with the whole that is always so much greater than the parts.

I remember learning more about the creative process on a week long retreat on the creative development through the lens of the tutor, Marie Beresford, than I had in all my years of writing. Although the creative process is organic, I learned to put handles on the process so that I was able to pan out from my personal experience and gain insight into the deeper layers of what was happening.

Because it was outside my familiar environment and the venue was set in idyllic surroundings, there was nowhere to go to escape oneself. We continually came up against our edges. Although we came together to discuss our various processes in a group setting, the main work involved sitting out in nature on our own and working with our creative problem. Many of us chose to shelter beneath expansive trees or spent the first few days sprawled out in the long grasses, meditating and making notes. We were fortunate to have perfect weather in July and the grounds were full of swallows scything and racing through the air as they swooped to catch the insects. The grounds were drenched from dawn to dusk with their excited chattering. When evening dropped gently into the grounds and the trees became silhouetted against the skyline, a shy deer or two would make itself visible and the sound of the resident owls echoed far into the night.

Despite our idyllic surroundings, though, each of us wrestled with our personal difficulties. The fact that we were all struggling despite the perfection of our surroundings quickly dispelled the myth that creativity can only be carried out in the right setting. So often we hear ourselves taking up the chant 'If only my surroundings were different,' or 'If I didn't have this job, or had more time, I would have the space to create.' Realizing that the setting has very little to do with the process is quite revealing and highlights the ease with which we all make excuses. I was aware of how distracted I became from my task; how it was easier to observe what was happening in the long grasses amongst the insect life, to holding the work as my prime goal. I had made copious notes, finding the preparatory process of amassing information relatively easy and wanting to get it over and done with. But I was also bored with it. Others from their individual feedback into the group were still struggling with the preparatory process, caught and imprisoned by their mindsets of perfection and how they thought their work should be. Much of the wrestling on a group level was mental in origin rather than emotional. And I learned that the need to keep everything on a purely mental level is a way of detaching ourselves from our feelings, both emotionally and somatically.

The exercises devised, when we were in the group, were ones which gently brought us in touch with our body and feelings, so it was possible to explore the creative process further. Several of the students acknowledged anger – with the tutor, with the venue, with the Summer School – saying that they hadn't wanted to come anyway and that they were only sticking it out because it was a requirement of the course. Still others felt that they had learned nothing and would have been better off staying at home and going to work and at least doing something 'useful'. These were all symptoms of the anxiety of what would be evoked within. All this was a perfectly natural reaction, we were assured.

This anxiety and fear underlies most of our manic defenses to keep ourselves busy in the known. It is not just that we have busy demanding jobs and lives; it is because we make it this way as a culture. We work harder and longer hours than ever, although financially we have never had it so good despite our complaints. Even our holidays are filled with business, one event tumbling in another, leaving us no rooms to manage our feelings and relax.

When we are no longer focused on activity, and the drive and purpose that fuels our everyday life is taken away, the mind and senses fall out of rhythm with the world. Feelings become overpowering and the driven exhausted body may set up its own defense mechanism by becoming ill so that there is at least something tangible to focus on.

After the novelty of rest or illness has worn off, which is very quickly, we struggle to force ourselves back into the well worked rhythm of endless activity. If we further deprive our senses of this, the mind goes into panic, throwing up all kinds of fears and frustration. No one enjoys this frustration period because it is so uncomfortable. After all, the whole of society is designed to keep us away from this frustration and abiding sense of helplessness. The advice here is to stick with it; to bear the intolerable uncertainty, knowing that this marks the gateway to another level of being.

Somewhere round about this point, something within us relaxes and gives up the struggle, like the imprisoned animal relaxes in the jaws of its predator, knowing that there is nothing more it can do but wait for an opportunity that may or may not present itself. As the voice of the world becomes silent, we become tired, sleepy and it is difficult to shake ourselves out of this.

We have reached the *Incubation* period, the third stage in the creative cycle, where the conscious mind turns away from the dilemma or problem and surrenders it to the unconscious. There is a sense of inner serenity, but also an acknowledgement that we cannot do any more.

When this specific stage was named, I hadn't been aware of what was going on inside me, except that I was incredibly tired and all the tiredness I had suppressed all year seemed to rise up and claim me. My time out in nature was spent dozing in the long grass or lying under a tree listening to the sound of the breeze stirring the leaves.

Carrying out further work on the project seemed impossible. I felt lazy, but just accepted it rather than fighting it. A number of other students on the course had been experiencing this too for the last few sessions, as if the process had decided to call the shots and we were powerless to resist. Some of us went for walks; a group of us one afternoon sought out the nearest beach and went skinny dipping in the water. This was very healing and there was very little sense of guilt.

The tutor talked about the importance of this incubation period as an opportunity for the unconscious mind to process data. Additionally, we had all been having very meaningful dreams.

Once the incubation period is accepted rather than fought against with self- punishing affirmations like 'I'm being lazy, I'm not doing enough', we can trust and accept it.

It is probably this stage that gives birth to the myth that artists and writers just lounge around ninety percent of the time, waiting for inspiration to come in! Although this is part of the truth, it is not all of it. This is why the artist and writer are working when they don't appear to be working; they have simply handed over the work to their unconscious. In this way he is facilitating the space for this, which is a task that involves huge levels of trust, since our natural impulse is to fill every available space with activity and noise.

Insight may kick in at any point during this period of unconscious turning. Suddenly, like a lightning flash, an important missing piece of the picture appears; the answer drops into place. This realisation, sometimes known as an 'ah-ha', may appear in a dream or emerge while having a shower a bath. It's like a bolt out of the blue and probably the most longed for and coveted stage of the creative cycle. It may have been this insight that first prompted us to enter the creative world in the first place, but until that flash we may have lost sight of it and doubted its validity. There is a real buzz with this feeling, akin to the athlete's high when endorphins are released into the system. There is a sense of relief with this and a deepening sense of trust which makes us more receptive and free to express itself. This euphoric feeling, like the blossom on the tree, rarely lasts long and it is important to take advantage of it while it is there, making notes, drawings, and creating music. However vivid the insight may be, once the conscious mind takes over, our senses become dulled again.

Working out is the stage following insight and grounds the abstract into matter. This is the marriage between the conscious and unconscious, when the two join or the unconscious hands the work over to the conscious mind. The insight will have released enough energy and enthusiasm to bring this into form and test out the ideas and put them into practice. It is also where the hard work begins again, as draft after draft of a book may be written and re-written. This is the final stage of commitment where inner trust needs to be strong enough to survive all the doubts of the worldly everyday mind. These doubts, however, are important too because they test the mettle of the idea and make sure it is sound and strong enough to withstand the initiatory fires that will give it a place in the world.

Very often, even if the frustration station is borne and negotiated successfully, we lose heart halfway through this final stage; it seems too much like hard work, we say. But our real fear comes from having our work – our baby – rejected, and this is the risk that we have to take amidst a culture that worships success and shuns failure.

The length of time that passes between the stages varies with everyone and although this model gives a shape to the creative process, it is not the creative process itself. It is intended only as a guideline.

The thing that I learned about myself was that too often I confused the *incubation* process as the completion of the creative cycle and moved from *preparation* and *frustration* to *incubation* very swiftly. When insight came it often took me by surprise which I suppose is its intention. Another common problem was that I focused too much on the result rather than surrendering to the unknown stages in between. Also I realized that I can experience several creative cycles simultaneously addressing different projects.

Others in the group admitted that they were unable to move out of the frustration stage for fear of letting go and losing control or other less visible reasons. Others wanted to stay in the incubation stage or got high on the illumination stage which is like falling in love.

The major handicaps to creativity are mindsets that we have

around it which may date back to our childhood and parental pressures; for example, my mother, an artist herself, was afraid of my not being able to make any money through my writing and pushed nursing as a much safer option. And this is modeled on our cultural mindset that you don't put any work into anything unless you get something out of it; i.e. money, fame and success. One of the mindsets that prevail is that writers make a lot of money! Less than one percent of published writers are bestsellers and although an artist may sell their work for a few hundred pounds it might have taken them several months to conceive and create it.

The true artist is in touch with his/her inner being and will endeavor to see what he/she can *bring* into the world, rather than what he can *get out* of it. The planet gives him life, food and a multifaceted backdrop of experiences to create from; he works in service of life as life works in service of him. The more we work along with the view that we have to get as much out of the world as possible, we become more and more impoverished as we cut ourselves off from the natural creative cycle and exile ourselves from our life purpose. Again we can see this in consumerism, where we stuff ourselves relentlessly in order to feel sated. Our hunger knows no bounds, because without purpose, which provides us with the valuable tools of service, we are eternally hungry and empty. And here I am not talking about the very real need to work to make a living; I am talking about greed!

Here I would like to mention that very often my ideas are conceived through an insight or illuminative stage. With plutonian energy the ground erupts in front of me and, like Persephone bending to pick the flower, I become carried away by a force of inconceivable power and passion. I fall in love with the idea and this carries me through to the first draft and I am loathe to make it ready to bring into the world, to leave my lover as it were and become grounded in the mess and confusion of everyday experience. In this I have blinded myself to the fact that it is in the mess and chaos of the everyday, that we meet our lover and become illuminated. Again, this evokes the image of the tree with its roots deep in the rich hummus of the earth, set against the bedrock of the living landscape, while its branches aspire to the endless vistas of the sky. The tree crowned in gold fire in the fall pays homage to the earth when its shed leaves decay to produce rich compost for its future growth. Within the tree, the sap rises in the spring and returns to the earth in the fall.

Time and time again I have found that the various stages of depression duplicate the cycles of nature and in my understanding of this I have found a map that defines a clear path through the wilderness. Understanding where one is in the process provides hope and insight where there was none before.

Part IV

Chapter 15

How to be with someone who is Depressed

One of the questions that I am often asked is simply: "How does one be with someone who is deeply depressed?" It is a question that I have posed myself as both a psychosynthesis guide and one who suffers from depression. I have found that, if anything, the more psychological knowledge we have, the further away we become from finding a way to be with depression. Here 'being' is the key word and theme. True being is a state of unconditional acceptance, of deep listening and empathy. True being can be so refreshing to someone profoundly depressed who may have had to suffer an endless litany of what they should be doing with their depression from well-meaning relatives and friends.

In order to know how to be with someone who is depressed, we need to examine and reflect upon our own way of managing, coping and, most important of all, being with depression in ourselves. Perhaps we have never been clinically depressed, but all of us will have experienced periods of disillusionment, disappointment and powerlessness within the face of a life event. How do we normally cope? Chances are we have our own tried and tested techniques of coping, dealing and living with the condition. Quite naturally we gravitate towards fixing, alleviating and comforting ourselves. The following exercise will enable you to find some ground around this.

Take a little time to go back to a period in your life when you felt total despair, powerlessness and hopelessness. Reflect upon your feelings at the time, how uncomfortable you felt. Then think about what helped you.

What didn't help you?

How do you look upon the experience with hindsight?

What did you gain from it, if anything?

How did the experience change you?

Now bring yourself back to the 'here and now'. Ask yourself, how this experience serves you now?

If you have had little or no experience of depression or feeling down, try to imagine that one day you woke up and, for no apparent reason, felt depressed. How would you deal with this?

You may react in one of several ways. What are these ways?

You might put your feelings on hold and concentrate on tackling the workload before you. This can sound strange, but denial is a defense mechanism that many of us resort to when we can't cope with something difficult. You might, if you have time, search back in your mind over the events of the last day to locate some sort of incident that might have upset or unnerved you. Perhaps you need to pan out and gain a wider perspective of your life. You ask yourself; have I been doing too much? Do I need a holiday? Am I depleted in emotional and physical energy? You might take yourself off for a walk, run, a visit to the gym or seek out the company of a good friend if this persists.

The purpose of this exercise is to look at how we individually respond to a period of depression, loss and despair within ourselves. How comfortable are we around it? Because how we react to depression in ourselves is precisely how we will be with others, even though this may be unconscious. There is no shame in not being able to be with depression, only in the denial of this. Depression is very much about what is unbearable and being with the unbearable takes enormous reservoirs of trust and courage.

We all have tools we use in the face of depression. These are ones to help us cope: tools that give meaning to depression, tools that treat, fix, alleviate and inform us about the condition, tools to distract us away from its intensity, tools to strengthen, to overcome, and to give us hope. The list is endless and although each approach is relevant within the treatment of depression, rather than enabling us to be with depression they can take us further away from the condition. The easiest thing to do is to rush to solution-based techniques, rather than staying with the discomfort and despair. And this is by no means advocating that we wallow in depression or revel in the symptoms but, before any real change can happen, there needs to be acceptance, preferably unconditional acceptance.

It is within this medium of acceptance that we can, ironically, change the situation. Acceptance creates a clear surface of being in which the tools of transformation can emerge, through the Self. In medicine, surgery or pharmacological treatment is recommended on the strength of a correct diagnosis; the problem or condition is diagnosed and then change that is resolution-based can be initiated. Sometimes the surgery or diagnoses may not, in the long term, solve the situation. Again, the condition needs to be accepted before it can be changed. And here there needs to be a distinction between acceptance and resignation that may masquerade as acceptance.

Resignation is a pushing down and a cutting off from a life force; in this there is no energy, just apathy filled with feelings of defeat and failure. Acceptance is an active participation. Resignation is inactive and somber; it can also become the breeding ground for deep resentments.

Too often, as a relation, a friend, therapist, or carer, we become *seduced* by the symptoms of depression, of which there are many. As we rush to attend to each of these, such as feelings of loss, despair, anxiety and symptoms of insomnia and loss of appetite, we effectively drown in the content. Submerged in the sea of symptoms and possible solutions we become increasingly drawn further away from *how to be with someone who is depressed.*

Content and information are useless unless they have a context to exist within. The context acts as container and guide, but the context has to be right. If we make depression our context then we become lost in the enormity of the condition regardless of whether it is triggered by biological factors, an emotional incident, or is hereditary. Instead, we need to reframe the context in the light of this book – depression as a spiritual journey.

Be aware of what happens when depression is reframed in this way.

The difference in texture is distinctly tangible. There is a sense of rightness within this context. Immediately, purpose and meaning are evoked. Holding depression in the context of it being a spiritual journey shifts the emphasis from being wrong and getting rid of to calling forth the qualities that the experience can *give* rather than the qualities it can *take away.* A subtle but profound change has happened: we have come into a relationship with depression in a new way. By surrendering our need to control, fix and overcome we have found the humility to *listen.*

But by holding depression as a 'spiritual journey' we open ourselves to a grave danger of 'spiritual flight' that we may be totally unaware of until it is too late. In maintaining a spiritual context it doesn't mean that we 'spiritualize' the experience and lose the valuable ground we have gained. We need to discriminate between spiritual context and spiritual flight, because the feelings of depression can be so unbearable we may push them down or try to rise above them which is resorting to flight rather than ground. In over-spiritualizing the experience we cut off our relationship with the one who is depressed, or the part of us that is depressed. In doing this, we may lose our humanness which is the very ground we need. The person who is depressed will know whether we are truly with them or not and in our innermost centre we will know also. Beware of the subtle way we can be captured by making depression spiritually exclusive.

Depression may not be alleviated for any length of time. It may reoccur cyclically in the person's life and despite all our sustained efforts to lessen the condition, the depression appears to be every bit as debilitating as before, perhaps even more so. We know that bodily illness can have remissions before reappearing again, like forms of cancer, heart conditions and various digestive problems. Even though drugs may alleviate the pain for a while, every now and then they seem to lose their efficacy, throwing the patient back on their own flagging resources again. But, even though the condition is resistant to long term treatment, the context remains the same.

Depression is perhaps the most socially isolating and hidden condition of our times. At the core of depression are profound feelings of disconnection from a social and spiritual network. Because of this, it seems ironical that a depressed person will choose to isolate themselves even more when they feel so alone. But, very often, the isolation is a protective one. The depressed person finds it very hard to be with themselves and senses the difficulty that others, even close friends and relatives, have in being with them. Social isolation may be the only way of maintaining one's self-respect.

Again the question arises: *How do we be with a depressed person?*

The answer here is within the concept of being (to be), rather than doing (to do). Within our Western polarization towards doing and keeping ourselves busy, exists a major deficit of being. Depression is all about being. As human beings we should know all about this, but we have forgotten, in our obsession with keeping active, how to be. Unless we can learn to be with ourselves through good and bad, with each other, we can never be fully present in a situation. This is because our energy is too polarized to panning back into past history to find solutions and causes.

Being is about dropping down. It is about breathing in, so that we can breathe out again. Focusing on our breathing is one of the first stages of awareness we learn in meditation. The moment our monkey mind runs off to be captured by some distracting thought, we quietly, calmly, bring attention back to the breathing. Try this little exercise:

How is your breathing now?
    Take time to explore this for a few moments.
    Is it fast? Shallow? Labored?
    How much are you keeping in your body? Keeping down, by not breathing?
    When were you last aware of your breathing? Was it earlier today? Perhaps it was yesterday or some day last week when we noticed we were out of breath or had a pain in our chest.

In Buddhist meditation, we breathe in and we breathe out slowly. We literally breathe ourselves into being. If we bring this awareness of breathing in and out regularly into our life, our meditation, if only for a few minutes at a time, there will be a moment when you will feel yourself dropping down, being the breathing, rather than doing the breathing.

I have found breathing is very grounding. It brings me fully into my body. It connects us with ourselves and also each other. Most of us spend the day living in the upper part of our bodies, mainly in our heads and guarding ourselves against the symptoms of unease in our solar plexus, experienced as anxiety or worry. If we had a mental image of our presence we would be squatting on our own shoulders, knees drawn up to our ears, as far away from the ground as possible. It is no small wonder that we suffer from headaches, excruciating neck pain and tension in our upper torso. I am reminded of how it feels to travel in one of those economy seats in a plane where there is so little room that my knees are closer to my chin than I would like and movement in the arms is limited to below the elbows. Two hours in that position can make me feel very cramped. Think about how cramped we can feel if we are psychically enclosed in such cramped conditions!

In the midst of most unpleasant or highly stressful situations we hold our breath and clamp our jaws shut, we cannot possibly be fully present most of the time. And here I want to return to the unbearable feelings of the profoundly depressed and ask again that question:

How can I be with this depression? Or this depressed person?

Somehow, the very asking of this question invites an answer; as the asking of a question opens up awareness and consciousness. Within the question is a peace that automatically and miraculously finds its own answer by establishing ground and presence. It is not that we lack the opportunity to find the answers we need. Rather it is because we have not learned to ask the *right* questions. Some questions cannot be answered in the normal cerebral way, because they have not been asked in that way, like the Arthurian Fisher King's timeless question related to the grail: 'Whom does it serve?' This question, received initially on the mental level, lingers in the soul and awakens consciousness.

'How can I be with this depressed person?' invites a totally different resonance to 'how can I help, fix or cure this person?' It is uttered with humility that invites the Self.

It is hard to have humility in the face of such a pervasive symptom where our cultural voice screams out: Cure him! Fix it! Get rid of the depression! I know this because I have asked this question in the midst of my most profound suicidal depression. I have asked it as a last resort when I seem to have exhausted every conceivable way of treating my depression and there has been nowhere else to go. And it is at this point, at the end of my tether, that I have felt the presence of the Divine or God. Opening to and experiencing that unconditional loving presence somehow finds the pulse of life within which is borne from the act of utter surrender.

I have found that there is so much about depression that resembles death. There is something terminal about the deeply depressed person: something that seems to suck the life out of everything that enters its domain, rather like a formidable black hole which is a star that has collapsed into itself, drawing everything into this yawning vacuum including time and space. In the midst of depression, like the snow witch in *The Chronicles of Narnia*, life becomes frozen, petrified and entombed within a prison of ice.

This is why many people find it hard to be with a deeply depressed person. How can one be with a black hole without being consumed by it? One of the factors that helps me here is that the latest in space research suggests that baby stars have an intimate relationship with black holes. In fact, Robert Roy Britt, Senior Science writer in the USA, referred to this as 'co-evolution' and in 2003 wrote: 'The cloud of gas that becomes food for a black hole also fuels the formation of new stars as the gas moves toward the centre of a fledgling galaxy.'

This, to me, is a beautiful metaphor for the hidden potential in depression and a model to hold for someone who is deeply depressed. It doesn't fix or solve anything, but cogently illustrates and accentuates the importance of holding depression in a much wider context. This is something you can do with a client, colleague or friend who is depressed and who cannot do it for themselves; know that their depression exists within a much wider context than the individual person you see. Remember how black holes give birth to baby stars; snowdrops emerge through the winter soil from darkness. Hold this vision. By doing this we can influence the person, the people we care about.

Chapter 16

Understanding Suicide

"I Have Lost my Angel"

I have lost my angel... I have lost my mind. The days are too long, too heavy; my bones are crushing under the weight of these days...

These words were penned by a young and talented journalist several days before she killed herself on the 29th of October 1995. She had suffered from deep unremitting depression for years and left behind a number of journals recording the desperate state she found herself in.

Earlier that month she had penned these words:

I will not last another month feeling as I do now. I do not question that my eyes are brown, and I do not question my fate: I will die a suicide within the next month if relief does not come relatively quick. I am growing more and more tired, more and more desperate. I am dying. I know I am dying, and I know it will be by my hand...

I am so bone-tired and everyone around me is tired of my illness.

Her body was found sometime later floating in a lake.

The sense that one has 'lost their angel' or lost that vital line of connection with their spiritual source is the overriding and persistent feature in deep and unremitting depression. We all know that as long as there is hope burning in the midst of an impossible situation that somehow things will get better one day, we can endure any amount of hardship. But once hope goes, life connection evaporates alongside it. Hope connects us with that potent energy of purpose, meaning and values, as the psychiatrist, Viktor Frankl discovered amongst his fellow inmates whilst a Prisoner of War in Germany. The sad thing about major depression is that it systematically wears away at this life connection of hope.

Shame

It makes sense that the more shame there is attached to suicide in a culture, the less it is spoken about and the more invisible it becomes. But despite the low profile of suicide, it still manages to leak into local and national papers on a weekly, even daily basis, often as a small 20 centimeter section to make up scanty news space.

At the time of writing this, a story has hit the national newspapers and made the front pages when a father leapt off a balcony in Crete taking his two young children with him. Tragically, the boy was killed in the disaster, while the younger sister survived with broken arms alongside the father who had multiple injuries. What makes this central news, besides the inclusion of the children, is the moving tribute from his wife, a nurse, in defense of him as a caring father. She quickly dispelled rumors that he had been drinking prior to the incident, and insisted that he had acted out of character with his usual self and that he should be monitored closely at the hospital as he was deeply depressed. It later emerged that in the last year, the father had lost two of his brothers through suicide. One of them had bipolar disorder.

This suicide closely dogs another incident where a young mother who, beside herself with feelings of despair around coping with her son's autism, threw both her son and herself off a bridge. It emerges through the stories filtering through the media over the last few days that she had been suffering from mental illness and had been deeply depressed for some time.

Suicide in the Young

What is hard to comprehend, given the relatively low profile coverage of depression among young people, is the actual enormity and gravity of this condition. In America, suicide is the third highest cause of death among young people. This moves up a notch when applied to college students. The statistics are alarming with suicide dwarfing AIDs and casualties of war. In the twelve years spanning the Vietnam War, over 50,000 were killed as a result war, but during the same time period there were 100,000 suicides in the States. And the single predisposing factor here was depression. In depressive illness cognitive functioning is impaired and judgment is dangerously undermined. In short, the severely depressed person cannot support or look after themself adequately.

Why then is suicide so prevalent in the young? Is it because of all the pressures that face a clever and ambitious person today or even a sensitive creative one?

For teenagers and those in their early twenties one of the main causative factors is that there has been no real experience of chronic depression to build up enough resilience and learn how to seek the right therapeutic intervention. Underlying most alcohol and drug experiences are profound feelings of despair, anxiety, alienation and isolation, all of which makes it hard for the young person to reach out.

In the UK alone, 140,000 young people find their way into A&E through suicide attempts. Even more do not even get that far. It seems ironical that AIDs and Alcoholic Liver Disease receive more publicity than suicidal people. Where a person suffering from AIDs has ongoing care, the suicidal and self-harmer will very often self discharge only to find themselves out facing the same stress triggers as before. Many parents will have no idea that their daughter or son has been so depressed that they have considered ending their life. I don't think this is because parents are neglectful, but rather the insight and thinking around this are too unbearable to allow in.

Suicide in the Elderly

Suicide among the elderly is even higher than among the young.

This, no doubt, receives less coverage because the elderly in our culture are regarded as having had their life and therefore not as important. This rather jaundiced and stereotyped outlook can be the very fuel that lights the fuse to suicide among the elderly depressed. This attitude is particularly endemic in our Western culture where suicide rates are the highest. Apart from depression being higher amongst the elderly because of ageing neural systems, other factors contributing to a suicidal choice are loneliness due to the death of loved ones and friends, ill health leading to a gradual loss of autonomy, lack of a social network and loss of prestige in the community. I have come across many elderly patients in hospital who are there because of a failed suicide attempt who will try and do it again because they feel they are a burden to younger family members rather than a resource for their grandchildren. The fact that suicide rates are so high among Western white males as opposed to older males in Africa, India or Asia speaks of our crumbling social infrastructure.

In the face of deep unremitting suicidal feelings and depression, as a society we are relatively powerless in knowing what to do or say. The whole subject is unbearable and leaves an uneasy feeling so that, if we are not closely related to the event, we might make a joke about it or change the subject. Relatives of suicides often feel doubly punished by the reluctance of others wanting to socialize with them and the ongoing feelings of extreme guilt and anguish over the loss of their loved one.

In the midst of this are unspoken mindsets that we carry

collectively as a culture as well as personally. And here it is worth looking at our own mindsets in relationship to these.

Mindsets about Suicide

- It is a selfish act
- It is a revengeful act, cool and calculating
- It is an easy way out – a coward's way
- It is the ultimate sin, tantamount to murder
- God will mete out punishment. It is unforgivable and past redemption

As a Selfish Act

Suicide is very rarely a selfish act, although it may seem that way to those left behind.

There are numerous case histories where people have spent weeks, even months wrestling with the impact on family and friends that such a debilitating depressive illness has. The depressed person may feel that in this final act of autonomy, he/she is releasing friends and family from the worry and responsibility of caring for him/her. Anyone who has ever lived with a profoundly depressed person for any length of time or anyone who suffers mental illness such as schizophrenia, self-harming or manic depression will know only too well how exhausting and trying this can be. No amount of love or care seems to help and, in fact, every effort made to console the sufferer seems to vanish into a black hole. Ultimately, suicide can be a relief to relatives and friends despite the feelings of profound guilt that such an act may invoke.

As a Revengeful Act

Again suicide is very rarely a revengeful act, but rather a desperate one. There may be anger at God or at oneself which may be directed openly towards others. I think most of us, if we are honest, at some point or other have thought of killing ourselves after a failed love affair, a huge disappointment, but that doesn't mean we are going to act on it.

As an Easy Way Out

There is nothing easy about suicide as the unsuccessful suicide attempts will support. It is messy and very rarely quick. I have seen too many patients, young and old, who have lost the use of their limbs through a failed suicide attempt or even become vegetables, unable to do anything for themselves. Suicide is not so much the only way out, but perhaps the only way out for someone who is tormented by relentless feelings of unbearable anxiety. There may have been weeks of premeditation – or a self imposed deadline: If things don't get better by such and such a time, I will end it. This 'bartering with God' is also part of the process most people undergo when faced with an incurable illness.

But also what needs to be remembered here is what may appear to be cowardice in one part of the world may be bravery in another part. For example, in Japanese culture, killing oneself in the face of defeat is seen as an act of ultimate bravery. This outlook doesn't make taking one's own life as a final act of autonomy as right, but rather provides insight into our cultural understanding of suicide.

As an Ultimate Sin

Who is making this judgment? God or the accuser acting as God!

This mindset is entrenched in powerful religious and cultural injunctions when suicide in many countries was a criminal act. In the 6th and 7th century, the Catholic Church took this to be a violation of the sixth commandment: 'Thou shalt not kill'. Suicides were not given a proper Christian burial or were interred at crossroads where they were not blessed or conse-crated in any way. Jewish customs forbade funeral rites, while

Islamic law regarded suicide as a crime as grave as homicide. In France, the suicide was dragged through the streets before being hung on the gallows. In Germany, corpses were put in barrels and thrown downriver so as not to return. Martin Luther proclaimed that suicide was the 'work of the Devil' and John Wesley said the bodies of suicides should be gibbeted.

To be fair these powerful injunctions were in place to strongly discourage others from following suit, because suicide can be contagious. There is evidence to support this in the suicides that will gather at particular spots and also following the death of an icon, like a film star, poet or politician, there will be a rise in suicide rates. As much as there is a public horror of suicide, there is also romantic idealization of powerful figures that may become heroes within the collective psyche. A longing for a better life in paradise can be a driving force and has been in the case a large number of people launching themselves into an active volcano at Mihara-Yama, a volcano on the island of Oshima, sixty miles from Tokyo. This began in 1933 after a young student became enchanted by a legend that purported to promise those who committed suicide in this manner would be instantly cremated and sent to heaven in the form of smoke. The story over a period of two years was to become a modern legend. It attracted 800 men and 140 women to take their life in this way in a desperate attempt to reach paradise before the authorities intervened and blocked access to the volcano. These were nearly all young people, disillusioned enough with their life to sacrifice everything in search of an idealized way to reach paradise. We will find threads of this idealization, this longing for a better life in the following section.

Suicide Bombers

We cannot look at suicide without including the troubled Islamic sector of the world. Fortunately, our understanding of the suicide bomber has been greatly enlightened by those writers and commentators who have lived in an Islamic culture and have some understanding of the religious and social pressures that face people who live in an occupied country, such as the Gaza Strip. Such a news commentator was Robert Baer whose 20 years in working for the CIA as Directorate of Operations, gave him a deep insight into the motives behind why young people should blow themselves up in a society so oppressed by occupation and where there is a lot of hatred towards the West. Giving up your own life may be the only autonomous decision that can be made as an act of supreme sacrifice to enable other's lives to improve. People sanction war which kills thousands for lesser reasons. He portrayed suicide bombers as intelligent, idealistic people who connected to an intensely religious cause where killing themselves for that cause would not only lead to prestige in the eyes of Allah and their country, but also earn them an honorary ticket to paradise. This obsession with paradise and celebrity masks a deep despair of the world they live in. The Gaza Strip is as far away from paradise as poverty is from riches.

One of the areas Robert Baer explored was the rise in female suicide bombers who he found were seeking to avenge their relative's death, as in the case of the 29 year old lawyer who blew herself up alongside 21 people. Her cousin and brother had both been tragically killed by Israeli occupation. Although she had studied in the West, she came from a background where there was little future for women who have already been abused. Martyrdom for a cause has been a childhood dream or ambition for these young women. What does this sort of suicidal goal have to say about the world these young people grow up in where this is the only way out of the living hell of their daily lives?

It is important here to differentiate between religion and spirituality as, sadly, the two often become conflated. Religion is a belief system that becomes out of control when it separates, divides, excludes and emphasizes difference. Spirituality is the connectivity that runs through all religions and all people.

Spirituality is the Grace that connects us. It is the light that shines through and includes all difference.

'If I had to live in that situation – and I say that advisedly – I might just consider becoming one myself,' Jenny Tonge, the Lib Dem MP, empathized. Her remark must have hit home somewhere as, after the Israeli Embassy expressed outrage at this, she was dismissed from her party's front bench. Indeed, in 2002, Cherie Blair remarked 'As long as young people feel they have got no hope but to blow themselves up you are never going to make progress...'

In the array of books and articles that have followed the London suicide bombings at least we are endeavouring to understand our adversaries rather than just condemning them. As the media zooms in on the individual lives of the suicide bombers and the unstable roots from which they have emerged, we are able to begin to comprehend the reasons why they acted as they did. Two ingredients work their common threads through the story of revenge and alienation: revenge for the massacre of cherished relatives and friends, and alienation from their homeland. Here the ground is shaky because of various powerful 'tribal' feelings evoked amidst this massacre of 'us' and 'them'. On this shaky ground, seeking to understand why a person acts this way may be seen as a gesture of acceptance. But the deed, that act of fear and desolation fuelled by desperation is not the person. The person is flesh and blood, connected with family and friends on one level, yet profoundly disconnected at another level. Only by endeavoring to understand can we build new ground and make sense out of nonsense.

This has everything to do with depression, oppression and repression. As the Indian prophecy says 'the sickness of a small sector of people mirrors a bigger picture of what is endemic in the culture'.

Chapter 17

How to be with a Suicidal Person

From Doing to Being

Again, in the midst of our endemic 'doing' and 'fixing' culture, we may feel powerless to help. And this is when we need to know how to be with someone who is feeling suicidal rather than doing anything with them or to them. It is the very concept of doing and fixing that creates a bigger gulf between those who are trying to help and the very private and untenable hell of the suicidal person.

Within the 'doing and fixing it' mindset resides the fear of our own powerlessness to alleviate the obvious hell the sufferer is enduring. In admitting our impotence we are being very human, because the more we pathologize and psychotherapize, the further we move away from our basic humanity. Empathy and sharing space with the suicidally depressed will have a much deeper impact than words. Often in the admission of ones own powerlessness is to walk beside a soul as a fellow traveler and a friend.

The best thing is to do nothing, but be with someone who is suicidal in much the same way as one is in learning how to be with someone who is depressed (see Chapter 16). There is an erroneous belief that getting someone to speak about their suicidal feelings will drive them over the edge. This is a myth. Dr Daniel Plotkin, a Los Angeles geriatric psychiatrist, says 'When suicide is brought up, it's a relief to the person contemplating suicide. It doesn't push them over the edge'.

I can firmly condone the importance of being with someone in their suicidal distress after experiencing this when I was deeply suicidal and talking to my therapist about my feelings. Having her sit with me in my desperation was one of the most healing and intimate moments in my life. There was no judgment, and what I can only describe as an all-embracing empathy which runs so much deeper than words. It felt as though an angel had come to sit by me in my time of darkness. In the mist of those moments of soul communication and understanding, another deeper presence seemed to enter into the space and this I can only call the Self.

Although there is training available in suicide prevention run by various groups throughout the United Kingdom and globally, it is something that we need to realize within ourselves. We all have access to this awareness. The only thing that stands in the way of it is our own fears which, in turn, are driven by deep societal injunctions and an overwhelming sense of responsibility.

The more we are able to get ourselves out of the way and be open to the other person not as someone with inconsolable, suicidal feelings, but as a fellow soul on the path of life, the more accessible we become to the energies of the Self which are endeavoring to emerge in our midst. It is absolutely essential that we hold the situation within the 'healing field', because suicide is often a desperate attempt to return to the Source, even though this may be wholly unconscious; deep down, the suffering soul has a longing for spiritual connection. Holding that connection for them may be the most valuable gift we can give.

Remember that the success is not necessarily in being able to talk someone out of suicidal distress, but in being with them in their place of distress. In this sense, it is more important to have shared that intimacy of communication than preventing them from committing suicide.

So to recapitulate some of these essentials in coping with

someone who is suicidally depressed:

What to do
- Never underestimate the value of a 'being with' consciousness rather than 'doing with' consciousness.
- Empathize.
- Questions open up consciousness, helping us to access levels of understanding that might not have been available before. Never be afraid to ask key focal questions such as, 'What is it like for you?' or 'Is there anything you need that I might be able to give or help you with?'
- Stay with the process and the discomfort you may experience around this. Remember those feelings of powerlessness you are experiencing may be what the suicidal person is experiencing themselves.
- Never underestimate the power of presence, of staying with the feelings that can be unbearable.

What not to do:
- To avoid facing the unbearable, steer conversation onto safer common ground, which will send client into not being heard, deeper shame and self-disgust.
- Fixing/mending/finding solutions
- Make comments like 'You have everything to live for.'
- Make the person feel guilty in an effort to manipulate the situation.

As a Spiritual Journey

Well-meaning friends have often said to me "At least you have a spiritual awareness. Surely that makes it easier?"

I have wondered about this.

On one level, having a spiritual awareness can, initially, lessen the burden of depression. But, after a while, mental and physical resilience wear thin over the years. Hope goes because the hope is in knowing that a condition is going to eventually pass or get better, and not worsen. Knowing and hoping that a situation or condition will ease is a lifeline. I have, as many have with a spiritual insight, believed that I was suffering from something I had perpetrated in this life or a past one. Rather than alleviating the burden of despair this belief may compound with the self-recrimination that can go on in the face of major depressive illness. And we have to remember here that most major depression is a bodily illness. It is hereditary and does undermine the healthy function of key parts of the brain. It is every bit as real and tangible as heart disease, diabetes or cancer. These conditions may, through correct treatment and healing get better, but they can re-emerge.

I have to say that in my deepest suicidal hours, which can be unremitting for days, to weeks, I have experienced the presence of God, of a great Love that in the words of the ancient hymn 'Will not let me go.'

Much later I came across a dear friend and colleague on my journey who would say 'It must be even harder for you to have the spiritual awareness and still go through this'.

Her words have often returned as a healing salve in time of profound inner darkness, not because of what her words meant or conveyed, but because she had thought about it enough to put herself in my position. She literally stepped inside my experience.

The biggest thing any of us have to deal with, in being with someone who is suicidally depressed, is our own powerlessness and fears around the situation. Once we have faced our own fears and powerlessness, we can relax enough to let our humanness show through and this is when 'presence' enters in.

The Gift
There is a deep and profound gift in having endured suicidal distress or even having made a failed suicide attempt. Because this gift emerges from the deepest wound within the individual

psyche it can be too painful too bear. This gift is the deep empathy and understanding which emerges from personal experience. It is a gift that is so terrifying to some that they split off from it to the point of condemning those who are suicidally depressed because the terror is in believing that it will pull them back to the awful place.

Being able to hold the cup of experience which has been won at considerable cost, is a sign that the fear has been faced and the split mended. Often those who condemn suicide most vehemently are those who are most afraid of harboring that impulse within themselves.

These dark experiences within the psyche need to be included and integrated properly in order to become effective therapeutic tools. Spiritual and psychological counseling is important here. Until a person can accept and include that dark wound in the psyche, the light that can shine through that wound, in being able to guide and strengthen others, cannot come into being. We cannot use what we split off from and exile from our consciousness.

I want to conclude this chapter with these words by Emmanuel, which were written in response to the question 'My brother committed suicide. What do I need to know about this?'

Your brother took his life and brought it Home.
Although the inadvisability of suicide is spoken of,
It is all right.

It is clear that when one chooses to quit school
It is necessary to come back again
And learn what could not be learned at that time.
I speak to you from eternity
And there is no limit
To the number of lives one can have.

Your brother is learning many valuable things.
He is Home. He is well.
He is working, and will design a curriculum
Next time that will be more compatible
With his willingness and his needs.

It is to yourself
that you must direct your attention.
What does it mean to you
To have a brother who killed himself?
You need to hear the voice of God within you
Which knows it's all right,
That he is eternal.
Hear the message he gave you.
No one eats alone.
No one acts in a vacuum. No one kills himself
Without leaving a legacy of growth behind.

Conclusion

If you have reached this far you might want to look at the notes and drawing you made in response to my chapter at the beginning of the book, *Asking the Right Questions*. And by the insights you have made through working with this material ask yourself the question: What has my depression given me?

You might want to make another drawing and, later, see how this compares with your first drawing and notes. Indeed, if reading this work has enabled you to ask the right questions and catch a glimpse of the light held within the darkness of depression or your personal treasure then I know I have made a good pass with the baton. For living with and working within the field of depression is a tremendous feat equivalent to an Olympic relay race or marathon. And participating in a marathon where great reservoirs of strength are called upon, it may be difficult at times to realize, let alone remember that the marathon is run in relationship with other runners and spectators cheering you on. Above all, as narrated in our worldwide mythologies, each marathon, whether it is in the form of a race, a work, a pilgrimage or an odyssey, comes under the influence of the Gods. And the Gods favor those who brave the elements and undergo ordeals and initiations, because they are creating the Herculean template to follow. But the heroes themselves, the pioneers of our history books and cyclical dramas, often experienced alienation from the Divine, and this, by far, was the hardest part of the quest: to keep the torch burning despite having lost sight of the wider picture. And yet, it is the very sense of experiencing this existential alienation from the Divine that we claw our way back to the realisation of our own innate divinity, albeit not always on a conscious level.

Finally, I want to stress that being on a spiritual journey is not exclusive to people who suffer from depression. We are all on a spiritual journey whatever our life lessons. Because the depressed can experience such a sense of spiritual aridity in the midst of their dis-ease, the need to see depression as part of a divine intervention to bring forth soul qualities, makes this sense of spiritual exile more bearable.

I want to close with the following poem I received many years ago in the midst of a very deep and extensive period of inner darkness. It was in those raw moments, before I finally began to emerge, that I felt the presence of the Divine – not coming from some remote place, but there inside the darkness and which I have come to know as the 'Light in the darkness.'

May I Ever Be Thankful

May my heart be too full of love to allow
fear and judgment admission.
Instead of feeling inadequate,
may I bear my lantern with pride.
Out of my inner pain, may I learn
to touch my fellow creatures with
healing fingers of compassion and understanding.
May the silent tears I have shed cleanse me
of all bitterness

Oh - Nameless One
Whose breath colours the dawn
and whose music spins liquid chords
across the most desolate heart.
May I ever be thankful...

Glossary

Amygdala: The amygdala is a small almond shaped structure, and it has been linked with depression as it is involved in emotional processing. People with depression have a smaller amygdala and this area is more active in the depressed person as it deals with fear and anxiety.

Being with: A way of entering the experience of someone, without seeking to label or change them, which involves unconditional acceptance of the complete person and Self.

Behaviorism: This is a theory of learning based upon the idea that all behaviors are acquired through conditioning. Conditioning occurs through interaction with the environment. According to behaviorism, behavior can be studied in a systematic and observable manner with no consideration of internal mental states or emotions.

Divine homesickness: A longing for one's spiritual home or connection with the Divine which may not always be conscious. It is believed to underpin a lot of the drug culture in the world.

Ego: An objective and topographical concept referring to a central organizing process that protects, defends and drives the personality. According to Freud, the ego is the part of personality that helps us deal with reality by mediating between the demands of the id, superego, and the environment.

Ego development: This is a process that begins soon after the infant is born and develops strongly throughout childhood. Healthy ego development promotes a balanced outlook and participation in life.

Eros: Greek God of Love, personifying the life force and sexual instincts. Freud contrasted this with Thanatos, the Greek God of Death.

Dr Bach's Flower Essences: These were developed by a London doctor in 1930 who left his practice to develop them. They consist of twelve flower and tree essences which, when ingested, bring about a needed change in personality. They support inner growth.

www.bachcentre.com.

Fisher king: This refers to King Percival in Arthurian legend. He had a wound on his thigh that never healed, and because of this, the land could not heal.

Gestalt: Gestalt is a German concept for 'whole'. This system of psychology and theory looks at the relationship between the parts, drawing them together in the 'here' and 'now'.

Godhead: In Judaism, this is the 'unknowable' aspect of God. This is distinct from the more manifest aspect. It is the ineffable womb from which everything proceeds.

Hippocampus: A part of the brain's limbic system which are a group of structures important to emotion, motivation, memory and spatial awareness. Depression and anxiety may inhibit the function of neural activity here. There is scientific evidence that anti-depressants promote the ability for the hippocampus to produce more cells.

Imprisoned splendor: A term used by Robert Browning to refer to 'the light within us all' which needs to be realized.

Intrapsychic: Our internal psychological processes.

Introjection: The act of taking in or ingesting the mindsets and beliefs of people around us. As children we do this quite easily until we have the maturity to make up our own minds. Even in adulthood, many of the beliefs we hold are other people's rather than our own.

Monomyth: A term used to describe the 'hero's journey'.

Matrix: Womb in which a concept or creative idea is embedded.

Moral imperative: According to Immanuel Kant, the moral imperative was a principle inside a person's mind leading him to act. It is also recognized as conscience and has divine origin.

Neurogenesis: This is the birth of neurons or nerve cells in the brain. It is said that greater neuronal growth takes place in the hippocampus, an area deep in the brain concerned with memory and learning. Antidepressants that affect the serotonin levels in the brain can be a precursor to their growth.

Peak experience: A level of consciousness where one feels at one with the universe. This relates to Maslow's work on self-actualization.

Progressive behavior: Ability to move forward and learn from an experience.

Psychospiritual: A form of psychotherapy that embraces spirituality.

Psychotic break: A psychotic break from reality where there may be hallucinations and delusional thinking.

Regressive behavior: Tendency to resort to old behavior patterns as a result of change, rather than move forward to embrace what is trying to emerge in the psyche.

Rite of passage: A ritual that supports a new way of life or being; for example, marriage, death and reaching adulthood.

Re-wounding: This means a tendency to repeat earlier conditions of wounding by putting ourselves in similar situations on a regular basis to become hurt. Until this becomes conscious it is hard to break this repeating pattern.

Shaman: A wise person or leader gifted with healing tendencies who can mediate between the spirit world and the mundane world.

Soul-making: The making of soul, through the hollowing out of life experience which lend depth and wisdom to our make-up.

Spinal Touch: A remedial form of Light Touch Therapy applied to the points and meridians of the back and neck. Its actions aim to restore the body's centre of gravity and alignment.

Superego injunction: This is the ego's critical and judgemental faculty, usually adopted from parental or other figures.

Thanatos: Greek God of Death. A term by Freud to describe the 'death instinct'.

World tree: Also called, Yggdrasil in Nordic mythology. This tree grows between Asgard, the realm of the gods, Midgard, the realm of humanity and Hel, the realm of the dead. It is this World Tree that the shaman would climb to find medicine to heal whoever came to him for aid.

References

Introduction

Alighieri, Dante, *The Divine Comedy*, Oxford Paperbacks, 1998

Evans, R, *A Psychospiritual Model of Suffering*, Institute of Psychosynthesis Training Manual Volume III, Edited by Joan I Evans, London, 2007

Fox, Mathew &, Sheldrake, Rupert, *Natural Grace*, Bloomsbury, 1996

Grof, Stansilav MD & Christina, *The Stormy Search for the Self*, HarperCollins, 1991

Harding, Esther, *The Value and Meaning of Depression*, Paper written for the Analytical Psychology Club of New York, 1970

Karp, David, *Speaking of Sadness: Depression, Disconnection and the Meaning of Illness*, Oxford University Press, 1996.

Some, Malidoma, *Of Water and the Spirit*, Arkana Books, 1994

Saint John of the Cross, (Sheed and Ward, London 1974)

Chapter 2: What is Depression?

Bunyan, John, *The Family Pilgrim's Progress*, Scripture Union Publishing,1983

Jamison, Redfield Kay, *Touched with Fire: Manic-Depressive Illness and the Artistic Temperament*, Free Press Paperbacks, 1996

Kramer, Peter, *Against Depression*, Penguin, New York, 2004

Manning, Martha, *No Place to Land*, Ballantine Books, New York, 2005

Sheldrake, Rupert, *Listen to the Animals*, Ecologist, 2005

Solomon, Andrew, *The Noonday Demon*, Vintage, 2002

Woolpert, Lewis, *Malignant Sadness*, Faber and Faber, 2001

Osho, *Tarot in the Spirit of Zen*, Gateway, 2003

Zeuss, Jonathan, *The Wisdom of Depression*, NewLeaf, 1999

Woolf, Virginia, *A Room of One's Own*, Penguin Classics, 2002

Chapter 4: The Meaning of Suffering

Buber, Martin, *I-Thou*, Continuum International Publishing Group, 2004

Cafell, Colin, *In Search of the Rainbow's End*, Hodder and Stoughton, 1994

Evans, R, *A Psychospiritual Model of Suffering*, Institute of Psychosynthesis Training Manual Volume 111, Edited by Joan I Evans, London, 2007

Frankl, Viktor, *Man's Search for Meaning*, Beacon Press, 2006

Karp, David, *Speaking of Sadness*, Oxford University Press, 1996

Moore, Thomas, *Care of the Soul*, Piatakus Books, 1998

White Eagle, *The Living Word of St John*, The White Eagle Publishing Trust, 2000

Wilde, Oscar, *De Profundis and other Writing*, Penguin Books, New York, 1973

www. Vatican.:Letter Salvifici Doloris, 11 February 1984

Chapter 5: Persephone and the Underworld

Assagioli, Roberto, *The Act of Will*, David Platts Publishing Company, 1999

Bolen, Jean Shinoda MD, *Close to the Bone: Life Threatening Illness and the Search for Meaning*, Touchstone, Simon and Schuster. New York, 1998

Campbell, Joseph, *The Hero with a Thousand Faces*, Fontana Press, 1993

Campbell, Joseph, *Myths to Live by*, Penguin, 1993

Chapelle, Danielle, *The Soul in Everyday Life*, State University of NY Press, 2003

Estes Pinkola, Clarissa, *Running with Wolves*, Ballantine Books, USA, 1996

Ferrucci, Piero, *What we May be*, HarperCollins, 1995

Frankl, Viktor, *Man's Search for Meaning*, Beacon Press, 2006

Hillman, James, *The Soul's Code*, Bantam Books, 1977

Hillman, James, *The Dream and the Underworld*, HarperPerennial, NY, 1979

Stewart, Michael, 'Persephone', *Greek Mythology: From the Iliad to the Last Tyrant*. http://messagenet.com/myths/bios/persephone.html (November 14, 2005)

Woolger, Jennifer and Roger, *The Goddess Within*, Rider Books, 1990

Moore, Thomas, *Care of the Soul*, Piatakus Books, 1998

Chapter 6: Tools on the Journey

Karp, David, *Speaking of Sadness*, Oxford University Press, 1996.

Kramer, Peter, *Listening to Prozac*, Fourth Estate Paperbacks, 1994

Kramer, Peter, *Against Depression*, Penguin Group, USA, 2005

Jamison, Redfield, Kay, *Night Falls Fast: Understanding Suicide*, Vintage Books, New York, 2000

James, Oliver, *Britain on the Couch*, Arrow Books, 1998

Nettle, Daniel, *Strong Imagination: madness, creativity and human nature*, Oxford University, New York, 2002

May, Gerald G, *Care of Mind, Care of Spirit*, HarperCollins, New York, 1992

May, Gerald G, *Addiction and Grace*, HarperSanFrancisco, 1991

Solomon, Andrew, *The Noonday Demon*, Vintage 2002

Wilde, Oscar, *The Picture of Dorian Gray*, Oxford World's Classic, 2006

Chapter 7: The Roots of Psychology

Assagioli, Roberto, *Psychosynthesis*, HarperCollins, 1993

Benson, Jarlath, *Old Wine in New Bottles*, Year Two Course Book. Published by Amacara Press for the Institute of Psychosynthesis, 1992

Dunne, Clare, *Carl Jung: Wounded Healer of the Soul*, Continuum,

London, New York, 2000

Frankl, Viktor: *Man's Search for Meaning*. Beacon Press, 2006

Jung, Carl, *Memories, Dreams, Reflections*, Vintage, 1989

Jung, Carl, *C.G.Jung Letters*, 1951-1961.V2, Princetown University Press, 1992

Post, Der Van Laurens, *Jung and the Story of our Time*, Penguin Books, 1978

Tart, Charles, *Beyond Ego*, From the book: *The Spirit of Science*, edited by David Lorimer, Floris Books, 1998

Chapter 8: My Journey into Psychosynthesis

Alighieri, Dante, *The Divine Comedy*, Oxford Paperbacks, 1998

Assiogli, Roberto, *Psychological Mountain Climbing*, Institute of Psychosynthesis

Manual, Amacara Press 2002, 65A Watford Way, Hendon, London, NW4 3AQ

Bailey, Alice, Teachings available from the Lucis Trust: www.lucistrust.org

Buber, Martin, *I-Thou*, Continuum International Publishing Group, 2004

Hardy, Jean, *A Psychology with a Soul*, Woodgrange Press,1996

Chapter 9: Going Deeper

White Eagle on Divine Mother, White Eagle Publishing Trust, 2004

Hillman, James, *The Soul's Code*, Bantam Books, 1977

Sutcliff, Rosemary, *The Wanderings of Odysseus*, Frances Lincoln Children's Books, 2002

Mascaro, Juan (translator), *Bhagavad-Gita*, Penguin Books Ltd, 1970

Chapter 10: Spiritual Emergency to Spiritual Emergence

Assagioli, Roberto, *Psychosynthesis*, HarperCollins, 1993

Caplan, Marian, *Halfway up the Mountain: The Error of Premature Claims to Enlightenment*, Hohm Press, US, 1999

White Eagle on Divine Mother, White Eagle Publishing Trust, 2004

Grof, Stansilav MD & Christina, *The Stormy Search for the Self*, HarperCollins, 1991

Lovelock, James, *Revenge of Gaia*, Allen Lane Publishers, 2006

Perry Weir, John, *The Far Side of Madness*, Spring Publications, CT, USA, 2005

A Course in Miracles by Foundation for Inner Peace, Penguin Books, USA, 2007

Evans, R, *Spiritual Emergency and Emergence*, Training Seminar, Institute of Psychosynthesis, 2004

Chapter 11 & 12: Dark Night of the Soul

Avilia Teresa, *Interior Castle*, Christian Classics, 2007

Campbell, Joseph, *Myths to Live by*, Penguin Press, 1993

St John of the Cross, *Dark Night of the Soul*, Dover publications, New York, 2003

May, Gerald G, *The Dark Night of the Soul*, HarperSanFrancisco, 2004

Fox, Matthew & Sheldrake, R, *Natural Grace: Dialogues on Science and Spirituality*, Bloomsbury Publishing PLC, 1997

Chapter 14: Treasure as Creative Process

Alighieri, Dante, *The Divine Comedy*, Oxford Paperbacks, 1998

Kramer, Peter, *Listening to Prozac*, Fourth Estate Paperbacks, 1994

Kramer, Peter, *Against Depression*, Penguin Group, USA, 2005

May, Rollo, *The Courage to Create*, WW Norton and Co, 1994

Shenk, Wolf, Joshua, *Lincoln's Melancholy*, Houghton Mifflin Company, NY, 2005

Russell, P & Evans, R, *The Creative Manager*, Josse. Bass Inc, Publishers, San Francisco, 1992

Chapter 16: Understanding Suicide

Baer, Robert, *See No Evil*, Arrow Books, 2006

Eldred John, *Caring for the Suicidal*, Constable, London, 1998

Jamison, Redfield, Kay, *Night Falls Fast: Understanding Suicide*, Vintage Books, New York, 2000

Marcus, Eric. *Why Suicide?* HarperCollins, New York, 2006

Frankl, Viktor: *Man's Search for Meaning*, Beacon Press, 2006

Conclusion

Rodegast, Pat. *Emmanuel's Book, A Manual for Living Comfortably in the Cosmos*, Bantam Doubleday Dell Publishing Group, 1997

BOOKS